THE SEARCH FOR THE PERFECT
CHOCOLATE CHIP COOKIE

Gwen Steege

WINGS BOOKS
New York • Avenel, New Jersey

Edited by Gwen W. Steege
Text design by Cindy McFarland
Copyright © 1988 by Storey Communications, Inc.

This 1994 edition is published by Wings Books,
distributed by Random House Value Publishing, Inc.,
40 Engelhard Avenue, Avenel, New Jersey 07001,
by arrangement with Storey Communications, Inc., Pownal, Vermont

Random House
New York • Toronto • London • Sydney • Auckland

Printed and bound in the United States of America

Library of Congress Cataloging-in-Publication Data

The Search for the perfect chocolate chip cookie/(compiled) by Gwen
  Steege
        p.   cm.
    Includes index.
    ISBN 0-517-10107-6
    1. Chocolate chip cookies. I. Steege, Gwen, 1940-
II. Title: Chocolate chip cookie.
TX772.S43   1994
641.8'654--dc20   93-42252
                                                           CIP

10 9 8 7 6 5

TABLE OF CONTENTS

THE SEARCH

Grand Prize
Junior League of Las Vegas   p.110

Finalists

THE SEARCH FOR THE
PERFECT CHOCOLATE CHIP COOKIE

"IF IT'S NOT CHOCOLATE, it's not dessert"—our family motto, succinct and absolute, has long determined the special occasion menu at our house, and surely we're not alone in our passion. Since its discovery centuries ago, the very word "chocolate" has immediately conjured up images and aromas of rich, thick sauces, elegant mousses, steamy hot drinks, moist, dark cakes, and delectable fudges.

Of the myriad inventive ways of using this superstar of ingredients, however, one of the most universally popular is that particularly American invention, chocolate chip cookies. Warm from the oven, they are the perfect offering to a cranky child, the supreme appeasement for a lover's quarrel, the ideal gift to a special friend, and the ultimate bedtime snack.

This last function struck the fancy of Chester Soling, owner of The Orchards, an inn in the Berkshires of western Massachusetts and part of the Chesterton Inns chain. In elegant, yet homey rooms, guests are offered fresh-baked chocolate chip cookies and cold milk by their beds every night upon retiring. In a search for excellence that characterizes all aspects of the inn's operation, Mr. Soling decided in early 1987 to sponsor a nationwide contest to find the very best chocolate chip cookie to serve his guests. The recipes in this book include the winners, as well as a selection of over one hundred of the other 2,600 entries that were received from almost every state as well as Italy, Canada, and Mexico.

To these winners, as well as to the many other contestants whose recipes are included here, I owe very special thanks. As they described to me how their recipe was special or how it had come to them, their warm and personal responses to this project made me feel that I had gained a chain of new friends all across the continent: thirty-eight states, plus Nova Scotia and Quebec, are represented here. Many shared family recipes, some of which were brought to this continent over a century ago. Others related how their experiences influence the way they think about food: an anthropologist teaches her children to consider where ingredients are grown and how they have come to be locally available; a wheat farmer's daughter from Saskatchewan, Canada remembers the magic that unrefined flour put into any recipe; a parent describes the enjoyment a batch of cookies brought in a Ronald McDonald House, a facility for critically ill children and their families.

I would like to express further thanks to Orchards Pastry Chef Heather Andrus, whose patient advice and guidance helped educate me to the many refinements of chocolate chip cookie baking. Two of Heather's own favorite cookie recipes are included on pages 6 and 12.

The chocolate chip cookie recipe each of these people has offered here has particular significance and appeal. How hard to decide which one to award a prize! As you bake your way through the recipes in this book, you may find your own special favorite, or better still, take off from these to create your own perfect chocolate chip cookie.

CHOCOLATE

THE ORCHARDS' CHOCOLATE-CHOCOLATE CHIP COOKIES

To transform these cookies into peanut butter chocolate-chocolate chip, the Orchards adds about 1 cup peanut butter to this recipe. Peanut butter should be creamed with the margarine before adding the sugars.

5¼ cups flour
1 cup, plus 2 tablespoons unsweetened cocoa
2¼ teaspoons baking soda
½ teaspoon salt
2½ cups margarine

2 cups granulated sugar
1¾ cups brown sugar, firmly packed
5 eggs
1½ teaspoons vanilla extract
2½ cups chocolate chips

Sift together the flour, cocoa, baking soda, and salt, and set aside.

In a large bowl cream the margarine with a wooden spoon. Gradually beat in the granulated and brown sugars, creaming until well blended. Beat in the eggs, one at a time, and the vanilla extract. Stir in the dry ingredients, combining well with your hands to avoid overmixing. Add the chocolate chips.

Drop by heaping tablespoonfuls onto parchment-lined baking sheets. Bake at 350°F. for about 8 minutes. Do not overcook. Place baking sheet on a rack so that air can circulate under the cookies as they cool, or slide parchment paper, with cookies still in place, onto racks to cool. When completely cool, store tightly covered. *Yield: 9 to 9½ dozen*

theORCHARDS

CHOCOLATE THROUGH TIME

IF YOU DESCRIBE your favorite chocolate dessert as "divine," you aren't the first to connect chocolate to the heavens. In fact, the evergreen trees on which the cocoa bean grows come from the scientific genus *Theobrama*, which translates from the Greek as "food for the gods."

Europeans first learned about chocolate in 1502 when Columbus brought cocoa beans back to Spain from his fourth and last exploration of the New World. A few years later the Spanish conquistador Cortez observed the Aztec emperor Montezuma and his household enjoying golden goblets full of a cold drink concocted of unsweetened chocolate, vanilla, and ground hot peppers. The Aztecs called this brew *xoco-latl*, meaning bitter water. It is said that Montezuma alone consumed fifty cups of it a day, while his large household downed another two thousand cups. Small wonder it was so popular, for the Aztecs believed *xoco-latl* bestowed energy, including sexual potency.

The Spanish improved the bitter chocolate drink by adding some sugar and a stick of cinnamon along with the vanilla, and so special was this culinary discovery that the recipe for processing cocoa beans was kept secret in monasteries for almost one hundred years. The secret was let loose when an Italian traveler smuggled some chocolate to the Italian courts, and by the mid-1550s, there were large chocolate factories in many southern European cities. From there the magic spread to Austria, France, and England, where in the mid-seventeenth century chocolate houses, like coffee houses, became favorite meeting places of the wealthy cognoscente. In France, King Louis XIV even established a position of Royal Chocolate Maker to the King, and Napoleon took chocolate along on his military campaigns for its quick energy value.

Chocolate was first manufactured in the New World in Dorchester, Massachusetts, in 1765, relatively late considering its growing popularity in Europe. Only a few years after that, however, it became an important substitute for tea when colonists sought to avoid the British tea tax, and Thomas Jefferson praised it as superior to both tea and coffee for health and nourishment.

Nineteenth-century inventiveness engendered first, in England about mid-century, a method for making a bar of solid chocolate, and then in Switzerland about twenty-five years later, a way of incorporating condensed milk into chocolate, thus producing milk chocolate. These innovations, coupled with the century's growing love affair with technology and machinery that made the large-scale production of chocolate possible, opened a realm of possibilities for the use and distribution of chocolate that seemed to know no end.

The United States is now the leading world producer of chocolate, followed by West Germany, the Netherlands, and Great Britain. Americans rank only seventh as world consumers of chocolate, however, eating a meager 10 pounds of chocolate a year, compared to an average Swiss who consumes 22 pounds. In the United Kingdom, each citizen eats 15.4 pounds and West Germans, 13.8 pounds each. It may be best not to contemplate the number of pounds we add to our own bulk by consuming 10 (plus or minus) pounds per year!

THE BIRTH OF CHOCOLATE CHIP COOKIES

It seems a long way from Montezuma's heady chocolate drink to American chocolate chip cookies. Appropriately enough from the point of view of The Orchards and their tradition of serving fresh-baked chocolate chip cookies at bedtime, these cookies originated in another New England inn, on the eastern side of Massachusetts, nearly sixty years ago. In 1930, Ken and Ruth Wakefield opened a restaurant in a colonial house in Whitman, Massachusetts on the heavily traveled road between Boston and the old whaling town of New Bedford. Known as the Toll House Inn from the early days when stagecoaches stopped there to pay toll at the gates, the Wakefield's restaurant was soon highly regarded for its excellent food and hospitable service.

Real fame came to the inn with Ruth Wakefield's impulsive invention of a brand-new kind of cookie. Like many serendipitous discoveries this one was quite simple. Having run out of nuts for a favorite colonial butter cookie recipe called *Butter Drop-Do's*, Mrs. Wakefield substituted broken bits of a Nestlé semisweet chocolate bar, expecting them to swirl into the dough as they baked and melted. But though they melted somewhat, they were still definitely little chunks of soft chocolate, and her new *Chocolate Crispies*, as she called them, quickly became a favorite with customers.

After the recipe was published in a Boston newspaper, the cookie so caught on with New Englanders that increased sales of Nestlé's semisweet chocolate bar in the Boston area caused Nestlé officials to investigate the source of the success. To make it easier to use their chocolate bars in the new recipe, Nestlé scored the bars so that they would break readily, and even invented and marketed a special chopper for cutting the chocolate up into the proper-sized pieces.

ORIGINAL NESTLÉ TOLLHOUSE CHOCOLATE CHIP COOKIES

2¼ cups flour
1 teaspoon baking soda
1 teaspoon salt
1 cup butter, softened
¾ cup granulated sugar
¾ cup brown sugar, firmly packed

1 teaspoon vanilla extract
2 eggs
12 ounces (2 cups) Nestlé® Toll House® semisweet
  chocolate morsels
1 cup chopped nuts

In small bowl, combine flour, baking soda and salt; set aside. In large bowl, combine butter, sugar, brown sugar, and vanilla extract; beat until creamy. Beat in eggs. Gradually add flour mixture. Stir in Nestlé Toll House semisweet chocolate morsels and nuts. Drop by level measuring tablespoonfuls onto ungreased cookie sheets. Bake at 375°F. for 9 to 11 minutes. *Yield: 5 dozen*

In 1939, the Nestlé company began making chocolate in the morsel form we are all so familiar with, and, after buying the Toll House name from the Wakefields in the 1940s, has ever since printed the original recipe on the back wrapper of the package.

The love and fame of chocolate chip cookies has spread far and wide since Mrs. Wakefield's fortuitous discovery in the early thirties. Surveys consistently rank chocolate chip cookies as the top favorite cookie of more than half, or even as high as nearly three-quarters, Americans, and facts and figures confirm these estimates with numbers that tax the imagination as much as those of the national debt or stars in the universe. For instance, more than a quarter billion pounds of chocolate chip cookies are said to be baked in homes every year: that's nearly 6 billion cookies! Laid end to end this would be enough to make ten rings around the earth, or extended into space, a single line of cookies would reach almost to the moon.

The American love affair with chocolate chip cookies has finally spread to Europe. In France, especially, American food, including the chocolate chip cookie, is "in." French cookie companies have recently been competing to produce the most authentic chocolate chip cookie, which is advertised on prime-time television in a typical New England setting.

In the United States, chocolate chip cookie stores have become an increasingly common business operation. There is even a publication available from a Los Angeles firm (American Entrepreneurs Association) on how to organize and operate your own chocolate chip cookie shop. Famous Amos was one of the first, but that enterprise has been followed by a series of equally successful competitors, among them Mrs. Field's and David's Cookie Kitchens. Although these now famous businesses are nationally known, small, sometimes of equally high quality, versions have cropped up all across the cities and small towns of the country. One of these, the Oh-Yum Chocolate-Chip Factory, operated by an enterprising 14-year-old girl and her 10-year-old brother, is represented in this book on page 89.

All of this interest has resulted in ever more exotic combinations of flavors and ingredients for our old favorite chocolate chip cookie. As Americans have become increasingly sophisticated in their taste for deluxe, imported chocolates, liqueurs, and high-priced nuts, such as macadamias, the chocolate chip cookie emporiums have attempted to meet or anticipate the demand. Once home bakers have sampled these wares, they have taken the tried and true, traditional Toll House Cookie recipe and sought to embellish and extend it to create their own surpassing cookie. The recipes that follow illustrate some results: you may now be the judge.

THE INGREDIENTS

THE ORCHARDS' CHOCOLATE CHIP COOKIES

6 cups flour
1 tablespoon baking soda
1 tablespoon salt
3 cups margarine
2½ cups brown sugar, firmly packed

1 cup granulated sugar
5 eggs
2 teaspoons vanilla extract
2½ cups semisweet chocolate chips

Combine the flour, salt, and baking soda, and set aside.

In a large bowl, cream the butter with a large wooden spoon. Add the brown and granulated sugars and continue creaming until well blended. Beat in the eggs, one at a time, and the vanilla extract. Mix in the dry ingredients, using your hands to blend well. Gently stir in chocolate chips.

Drop by heaping tablespoonfuls onto parchment-lined baking sheets. Bake at 350°F. for about 8 minutes. Do not overcook. Place baking sheet on a rack so that air can circulate under the cookies as they cool, or slide parchment paper, with cookies still in place, onto racks to cool. When completely cool, store tightly covered. *Yield: 9 to 9½ dozen*

theORCHARDS

WHAT COMES OUT DEPENDS ON WHAT GOES IN

BEFORE BREAKING OUT the pans and diving into the chips, some words should be said about ingredients and about mixing, baking, and storing your chocolate chip creations. Although there are surprising, in fact almost infinite, variations in just this one kind of cookie, there is a basic precept you should always keep in mind: *the quality of the result is determined first, by the quality of what goes in, and second, by the care with which you handle the ingredients*. Always use the freshest and highest quality ingredients you can find, and then treat them with respect when you store, sift, chop, measure, beat, and bake them.

To be honest, the lists of ingredients for almost all the recipes in this book bear some striking similarities to one another. Many are, in fact, based more or less closely on that original Toll House Cookie recipe that Mrs. Wakeman and then Nestlé made famous and beloved. In addition to chocolate chips, they usually include butter, margarine, or shortening; brown and/or white sugar; egg; all-purpose flour, alone or in combination with other kinds of flour and grains; baking powder and/or soda; flavoring; and sometimes nuts. The intriguing thing is that within these few food groups, there are still many choices related to proportions and techniques and specific ingredients, each of which will produce a significantly different cookie. Small changes here and there, inspirations about new flavors to incorporate, and *voila*, a wholly new variation on the old theme.

The very best way to begin your own search for the perfect chocolate chip cookie is to try to understand a bit more about the basic ingredients that are most commonly found in cookie making. Consider what they are, what their roles are in the basic dough, and how they should be handled, and then try them out in your own test kitchen.

First, and most especially, let's begin with the chocolate.

CHOCOLATE

Chocolate was brought to Europe at the beginning of the sixteenth century by Columbus, and the process for producing something wonderful from those unpromising little seeds of the cacao tree was kept secret for many years. The technology of chocolate making is still considered one of the most complex. Grown only in tropical climates, mostly in West Africa and Central and South America, the cacao tree must be eight years old before it produces a fruit, or pod, about the size and shape of a summer squash. Each tree produces twenty to forty pods, filled with twenty-five to fifty, one-inch, almond-shaped, creamy violet seeds or beans. These beans are sun-dried, fermented, cleaned, blended (like coffee or wine growers, each manufacturer has a special formula for a blend of beans from different countries and different varieties of cacao trees), roasted to bring out their flavor and aroma, and hulled.

When the beans are crushed between stones or steel blades, they generate heat and liquefy, allowing the *cocoa butter*, or cocoa fat, to be extracted under pressure. Cocoa butter is what allows chocolate to melt; it also gives chocolate its special creamy texture. The thick, dark paste that remains after most of the cocoa butter is removed is called *chocolate liquor*. The beans usually yield about equal amounts of cocoa butter and chocolate liquor. From this point any of the various kinds of chocolate called for in cooking and baking can be made, depending upon the percentage of pure chocolate liquor in relation to other ingredients, such as reintroduced cocoa butter, sugar, and milk.

Sweetened chocolate undergoes two additional steps: refining, which reduces it to a paste, and conching, which assures the smoothness of the finished product—the longer the conching period, the smoother, and also the more expensive, the chocolate. An aging period of up to six months further improves flavor.

In American-processed chocolate, the remaining product after most of the cocoa butter is removed is *cocoa powder*. This is lower in fat than any other kind of chocolate (about 10 percent cocoa butter remains) and, if stored airtight, will stay fresh and of high quality almost indefinitely, even without refrigeration. *Breakfast cocoa* has a higher fat content (at least 22 percent). *Dutch-processed cocoa* is treated with a very small amount of alkali, which neutralizes the acids in the liquor and makes the chocolate darker and less bitter than American-processed cocoa; it also blends more readily with liquids. If you use cocoa as a substitute for baking chocolate in cookie recipes, its flourlike consistency may result in a cakier cookie. Bitter or *baking chocolate* is also pure chocolate liquor, with most of the cocoa butter removed. In this case, the liquor is cooled and molded into blocks, 1 square or block equaling 1 ounce.

Instant cocoa contains sugar and dry milk solids for quick convenience in mixing chocolate-flavored drinks. It is an entirely different product from plain cocoa, therefore, and should not be substituted in baking for other kinds of chocolate.

Semisweet chocolate, the kind most commonly packaged as chips and thus the star ingredient of this book, contains at least 35 percent pure chocolate liquor, plus some cocoa butter added back in along with sugar and vanilla, while *bittersweet chocolate* is 50 percent pure liquor, with less sugar than semisweet. In *sweet dark chocolate*, the proportion of pure liquor goes down to 15 percent, with a higher amount of sugar. *Milk chocolate* contains at least 10 percent chocolate liquor and about 16 percent milk, cream, or dry milk solids as well as cocoa butter, sugar, and flavorings. *White chocolate*, or confectioners' chocolate, contains no chocolate liquor, and thus by law is not chocolate at all. It is made by cooking down milk and sugar until they are almost solid and then adding cocoa butter and vanilla.

Be on guard against products labeled *artificial chocolate*, which may actually contain no chocolate at all. Often some or all of the cocoa butter is replaced by ingredients that give the chocolate a waxy texture. *Chocolate flavored* means something slightly different. Chocolate-flavored products do not have enough pure chocolate to meet government standards for real chocolate and may contain vegetable oils and other additives, as well. Premelted liquid chocolate packaged for baking convenience and chocolate syrups fall into this category. Neither the taste

COCOA AS A SUBSTITUTE

Cocoa can be substituted for other kinds of chocolate using the following proportions:

3 tablespoons cocoa plus 1 tablespoon butter, margarine, or shortening	= 1 square of baking chocolate
6 tablespoons cocoa, 7 tablespoons sugar, and ¼ cup butter, margarine, or shortening	= 6 ounces (1 cup) semisweet chocolate chips
3 tablespoons cocoa, 4 ½ tablespoons sugar, and 2 ⅔ tablespoons butter, margarine, or shortening	= 4 ounces of sweet baking chocolate

nor the texture of imitation chocolate matches the real thing. Your final cookies will be only as good as what goes into them, and using inferior quality ingredients, especially the lead player, chocolate, will result in inferior cookies.

STORING CHOCOLATE

Chocolate has a long shelf life: milk chocolate is good for about six months, and dark chocolate for well over a year in a cool (about 60°F. to 75°F.), dry place. In fact, many people feel that good chocolate, like fine wine, improves over a period of many years.

Temperatures above 78°F. will cause the chocolate to begin to melt and the cocoa butter to begin to separate out. Similarly, moisture can cause the sugar to melt and condense on the surface of milk or semi-sweet chocolate. When either of these happen, a grayish-white film may develop on the outside of the chocolate. This film, which is called *bloom*, is harmless, though not aesthetically appealing, and will not affect the taste or quality of chocolate used in baking. Chocolate may also be frozen; all kinds keep for about a year in the freezer. Please note, however, that chocolate that has been frozen is perfectly acceptable for use in baking, but if you are planning to use the chocolate for anything more complicated, such as candy making, it is best not to freeze it.

Cocoa keeps its freshness and quality almost indefinitely without refrigeration, but it, like all other chocolates, should be kept tightly wrapped so that it won't absorb odors and moisture. If chocolate is frozen or refrigerated, bring it to room temperature, in its wrapper to avoid sweating, before using in baking.

MELTING CHOCOLATE

Chocolate should be treated with respect while melting it, for it has some funny ways if not handled properly. For quick, even melting, break or chop the chocolate into small pieces with a chef's knife, or grind in the blender or food processor before placing over heat. The safest way to melt all kinds of chocolate is to place it in the top of a double boiler over hot, but not boiling, water. This way you will not have to worry about scorching it or getting steam into it. If you attempt to melt it over direct heat, be sure to use very low heat and a heavy saucepan, and stir it constantly. Very small amounts can be melted in a heatproof cup placed in a pan of hot water.

If you use care, microwaving can be a satisfactory way of melting chocolate. Unwrap and chop blocks of chocolate and place in microwaveable cup or bowl. With microwave set at 500 watts, microwave for 1 minute, checking after 30 seconds. Stir with a rubber spatula to encourage even melting, then microwave for another minute, again checking after 30 seconds. Allow chocolate to stand and complete melting for several minutes and stir again. You may need to return chocolate to microwave for an additional 30 seconds if some lumps still remain. The length of time necessary varies with the amount of chocolate you need to melt. Be careful not to microwave too long, however, or chocolate will harden and burn.

Too high temperatures or moisture from steam or wet utensils may cause the chocolate to become stiff, grainy, and unworkable. This dismaying event is called *seizing* and can sometimes be remedied by vigorously beating in 1 teaspoon solid vegetable shortening (do *not* use butter, which, because it contains water, may worsen the problem) for every 2 ounces of chocolate. Seizing can be avoided by melting a couple of tablespoons of another ingredient from the recipe, such as butter, along with the chocolate.

If melted chocolate cools too much and hardens before you have a chance to incorporate it into your dough, it may be reheated using the same precautions as for first-time melting. Always be careful not to allow chocolate to get too hot: it burns very easily.

WHAT KIND OF CHOCOLATE SHOULD YOU USE?

Take time to enjoy experimenting with various sized chocolates now available, from minichips, which assure a tiny bit of chocolate well dispersed throughout the cookie, through maxichips and chocolate chunks, right up to pieces of candy, such as Hershey's Kisses or M&Ms. Consider what you want the cookie to feel like when you bite into it: minichips may melt into and get lost in the dough while baking and maxichips are just too much chocolate for some people's idea of a cookie. If none of what's on the grocery shelf seems just right, you have the whole world of chocolate bars, right up to the most prestigious imports, to experiment with.

The choice of what kind of chocolate you should use is really limited only by your own taste. Have a chocolate-tasting session—that shouldn't be an onerous chore! Buy several different brands, including your supermarket's "generic" brand, and also sample different kinds of chocolate: bittersweet, semisweet, milk, and sweet. Number them and keep a list separately so that you won't know the kind or brand you are sampling and thus have preconceived notions of what is best. Then set yourself the task of ordering them by your preference. Smell them, taste them, let them melt in your mouth a bit, then drink a bit of water and wait awhile before moving on to the next so that you can really savor each one individually. Judge the relative smoothness or graininess, sweetness or bitterness, the waxiness or creaminess of each chocolate. Each manufacturer's recipe for processing and mixing chocolate is different, and their products are therefore distinctly different as well.

This blind approach may offer some surprises, and it certainly will be fun. The most expensive, imported chocolate may not, after all, be the one you choose over more readily available, less expensive kinds. Orchards Pastry Chef Heather Andrus finds the generic or the commonly available brands and regular-sized semisweet chocolate chips to be good for a delicious, traditional cookie.

If you can't make up your mind, try combinations of two or more chocolates, such as white, milk, and semisweet chocolate. You will find that the variety adds texture as well as flavor to the cookies. When you make chocolate chip cookies, look for recipes in this book that use your favorite types, or substitute what you like best for what is called for in the recipe—the first step in inventing your own special recipe.

Once you have the hard decision of what kind of chocolate to use out of the way, you are ready to deal with the basic dough of the cookie itself. Two important components determine the tenderness of the cookie: butter/margarine/shortening and sugar.

BUTTER, MARGARINE, OR SHORTENING?

There are excellent cookie recipes calling for either butter or margarine, as well as shortening, or even, occasionally, vegetable oil (never substitute oil for butter or shortening). Each produces a significantly different flavor and texture, however, and thus each has strong advocates. Often recipes call for more than one in an attempt to get the best of several worlds. The temperature of these ingredients affects the result, too, and although usually butter or margarine should be room temperature before using, some recipes require chilled or even frozen butter, while others call for melting the butter first.

Some recipes in this book leave the choice of whether to use butter or margarine up to you, but in those recipes that call for butter, the special flavor and texture butter lends were particularly important to the recipe's creator, and your results will be slightly, or in some cases substantially, different if you make substitutions. Generally speaking, margarine improves the texture and butter improves the flavor of cookies. Butter also tends to make a crisper cookie. Butter and margarine are often used in equal parts in chocolate chip cookie recipes. Do not, however, use whipped margarine, which has added water and does not do for the dough what regular margarine or butter does.

Remember that, although butter lends a wonderful flavor to baked goods, it also produces a cookie that spreads and burns more quickly, so watch butter cookies extra carefully while baking, particularly if the butter (or margarine) is a bit too soft to begin with.

Many of the recipes that follow call for unsalted, or sweet, butter. In the days before adequate refrigeration, salt was used as a preservative in butter. Nowadays, because different brands vary in saltiness, many cooks prefer using unsalted butter in order to regulate the salt better in their baking. And many cooks simply prefer the smooth taste of unsalted butter. It is safest to make no substitution when a recipe calls for unsalted butter, or at least to reduce the amount of salt somewhat if you must use salted butter or margarine.

Pure, solid, all-vegetable shortening is also quite good in cookie baking. Vegetable shortening is the result of hydrogenating, or adding hydrogen, to vegetable oils, such as polyunsaturated soybean, palm, and sunflower oils. Compared to butter, shortening produces softer, spongier textures in baked goods. A cookie made with shortening is a "short" cookie—one that breaks solidly and thickly, like a peanut butter cookie or shortbread, rather than with a snap. You may like a combination of shortening and butter. When substituting shortening for some or all of the butter or margarine in a recipe, cut the amount by about one-fifth.

SUGARS

Sugar is present in cookies not only to sweeten the dough but to make it more tender. In this book when the word "sugar" alone is listed, use white, granulated sugar. Many chocolate chip cookie recipes call for brown sugar as well as granulated sugar. Both light and dark brown sugars are available. Added molasses gives dark brown sugar its color and stronger flavor. The term brown sugar alone in recipes usually refers to light brown sugar, though your own preferences may dictate which kind of sugar you use.

Brown sugar will harden to stone if not stored in a tightly closed container. To further ensure against hardening, place a piece of bread in with the sugar; do not use highly seasoned bread, however, or it will "share" its flavor with the brown sugar. Brown sugar may be softened by placing it in a shallow pan, misting it with a small amount of water, and putting it in a 300°F. oven for 15 minutes or so until it has improved. If you have a microwave oven, place the sugar in a shallow dish and put both the dish of sugar and a small bowl or cup filled with water in the microwave. Microwave for about 3 minutes on high. If the sugar has not improved, continue microwaving for 1 minute at a time, checking the softening progress after each minute. Even very hard sugar should respond to either of these treatments.

Unlike most other ingredients, brown sugar should always be packed firmly down into the cup when measuring.

Corn syrup is thought by some cooks to produce a chewy cookie with a crisp outside. Since these are often much sought-after characteristics in a chocolate chip cookie, try some of the recipes in this book that use corn syrup (see index) to see if you agree. Usually only a few tablespoons of corn syrup substi-

tute for part of the sugar in a recipe.

Honey may also be used as a sweetener, in substitution for all or part of the sugar. Use about three-quarters the sugar measurement you are substituting for, and cut back on the amount of liquid in the recipe. This may take a bit of experimentation before you get it right. Cookies with honey will be more moist and softer than those made with sugar.

EGGS

Eggs should always be as fresh as possible, as long as they are, somewhat contradictorily, at least three days old. Eggs contribute to the moistness, lightness, and tenderness of a cookie. The process of creaming the butter and sugar and then beating in the eggs incorporates air into your cookie batter and assures light, tender cookies. The fresher the eggs, the more air that can be beaten in. Room temperature eggs can also be beaten to greater volume. Most of the following cookie recipes do not require that the eggs be beaten before being added to the butter and sugar.

Unless otherwise noted, use large, Grade A eggs. Brown or white are equally fine, as long as they are quite fresh.

VANILLA EXTRACT

Vanilla was first brought to Europe from the court of Montezuma by Cortez. The cured fruit of a tropical orchid, most vanilla used in the United States today comes from the island of Madagascar.

It's much nicer to use real vanilla extract rather than imitation vanilla flavor in baking. Although the extract may seem rather expensive, you really don't use that much in any one recipe, so your investment will last a fairly long time. If you are going to the trouble of having all your other ingredients fresh and wonderful, why spoil the whole thing with imitation flavor?

It's quite simple as well as less expensive to make your own vanilla extract. Split three or four vanilla beans lengthwise, cut them into 3-inch pieces, and place them in a pint of light rum, tightly corked, for at least a month before beginning to use—the longer you can wait, the better the flavor. And the brew smells marvelous!

FLOURS

In the following recipes when the word "flour" alone is listed, use all-purpose, unbleached wheat flour—all-purpose, because its mixture of hard, high-gluten and soft wheats is best suited to cookie baking, and unbleached, because it is of higher nutritional value. All-purpose flour has had both the outermost part of the grain seed, the bran, and the innermost germ removed during the milling process. The flour is then enriched by reintroducing some of the vitamins and minerals lost with the bran and germ. The result is a smooth white flour that both stores better and pro-

duces lighter baked goods than whole wheat flour.

The moisture content of different brands of flour varies somewhat, thus affecting the amount of liquid required in a recipe. You may need to add a bit more or less flour to a dough to compensate for differences in absorption or the relative humidity in your kitchen. Knowing whether and how much to change a recipe comes with experience and experimentation.

Unless specifically noted otherwise, because stored flour settles, it should be sifted before measuring, not to rid it of lumps or impurities, but to "unsettle" it. For this reason you may wish to sift even whole wheat flour, and then add back in the particles that do not go through the sifter. To measure flour, spoon it lightly into a dry-measuring cup (a graduated cup available in nested sets of ¼, ⅓, and ½ cup sizes). Carefully level off the excess at the top with a knife, being careful not to pack or shake down the flour in the process. Finally, add the other dry ingredients, such as baking powder or baking soda, salt, and spices, to the sifted flour, and sift the whole thing again to blend everything well. To save clean-up time, do this sifting operation onto large squares of waxed paper.

Some cookie recipes call for cake flour, which is made of soft wheats with less gluten and which produces cookies of a more crumbly texture than those made with all-purpose flour. If you wish to substitute all-purpose flour for cake flour, use 2 tablespoons less per cup. Be aware that the results still may not be quite the same as if you used cake flour.

Bread flour is made from hard flours with a higher

proportion of gluten. The resultant dough is apt to be elastic and produce a rather tough cookie. As with other ingredients with alternative possibilities, it is interesting to experiment with different kinds of flours for different effects.

Many cookies get an extra boost of flavor, texture, and nutrition from the incorporation of whole wheat flour, wheat germ, or bran, as well as other grains such as oatmeal, along with all-purpose flour. A good way to get a secret infusion of good nutrition into your children is by smuggling a bit of soy flour (high in iron, calcium, and protein), bran (fiber), or wheat germ (nutty flavor, combined with good protein and mineral content) into their snacktime cookies. You don't need to add much of any of these to increase significantly the nutritional value of your cookies. The recipes on pages 87–108 are good examples of how well these ingredients work.

Rolled oats are a favorite ingredient for cookies and are found in many of the recipes in this book. You will find both regular and quick-cooking oats on the grocery shelves. Do not use instant oatmeal; it has been processed and added to until it has been deprived of the nutty flavor and texture of natural rolled oats. Whether to use quick-cooking or regular oats is a matter of preference. Quick-cooking oats have thinner flakes and blend more completely into the cookie dough, while regular oats retain their shape and chewiness. Cookies made with regular oats will be crunchier and more crumbly, like granola bars.

For extra nuttiness and crunch, try lightly toasting rolled oats before using them in baking. To toast oats, spread them in a large baking pan and bake them in a 325°F. oven for about 15 minutes, watching and stirring them frequently to avoid burning them.

Some recipes call for oat flour, which can be made by whirling oats in the blender or food processor until they are reduced to a fine powder. Part oat flour in a recipe will yield denser, thicker cookies.

It is even possible to use part cornstarch in place of some of the flour in cookie recipes. This produces a wonderfully crisp cookie. In Great Britain, corn flour, which is quite similar to cornstarch, is used in shortbread.

LEAVENING

If we put no leaven in the form of baking powder and baking soda into our cookies, we would end up with hard, unappealing rocks, instead of tender, crumbly pastries. Leaven is another way of incorporating air and lightening the dough, in addition to the process of creaming the butter, sugar, and eggs.

Both baking powder and baking soda contain an alkaline and an acid that react with each other when moistened to form carbon dioxide gas. The gas makes little bubbles in the dough that expand under the heat of baking and leave little air pockets all through the cookies after they cool, thus producing crumbly, light cakes and cookies.

Double-acting baking powder is most commonly used in cookie baking. A combination of cream of tartar, bicarbonate of soda, and salt, it is referred to as double-acting because it begins its work even in the cold dough, though most of its action takes place while the cookies are baking.

Some recipes call for a small amount of baking soda in addition to the baking powder. Baking soda tends to produce an even tenderer cookie. It works only in the presence of an additional acid, such as sour cream, buttermilk, or molasses. When you use baking soda alone as leavening, get the cookies into the oven as quickly as possible. Since it is single-action only and begins to work as soon as moisture hits it, it may lose its power before the heat can set the air pockets. The result will be hard, flat cookies.

Both baking powder and baking soda should be well mixed with the flour in the recipe before adding to the moist ingredients.

NUTS

One of the most controversial of chocolate chip cookies ingredients, nuts have staunch advocates of and fierce opponents to their presence in chocolate chip cookies. A recent survey found that two-thirds of Americans preferred their chocolate chip cookies without nuts, yet the flavor, texture, and nutrition that nuts offer all continue to tempt cookie bakers to try different kinds in their recipes. One Orchards contestant suggested grinding walnuts or almonds rather finely to get a nutty flavor without adding the lumpiness of nuts that offends those anti-nut people among us. Conversely, some folks would prefer not even to chop the nuts, but simply break the pieces up rather coarsely with their fingers.

To enhance their flavor, some nuts, such as hazelnuts (known as filberts in some parts of the country), should be lightly toasted before using in baking. Spread them thinly and evenly in a large baking pan, and place in a low oven (about 300°F to 325°F.) for about 15 to 20 minutes. Stir them frequently and watch them carefully to avoid burning or toughening the nuts by overcooking.

Nuts chop more easily if warm and moist. Both shelled and unshelled nuts keep best (up to a year) frozen.

These then are the basic ingredients of chocolate chip cookies. As has been noted, even without adding anything else, variations in their proportions and specifics make striking differences in the outcome. To further enhance or, perhaps more accurately, to gild the lily, the list of other possible ingredients is limited only by your taste and imagination. The recipes that follow are embellished with extra chocolate, pinto beans and zucchini, coconut and all kinds of nuts, oranges and apricots, Irish Mist, crème de menthe, and other liqueurs, among other interesting ideas. Look for your favorites and then let yourself be inspired to inventiveness.

MIXING

CHOCOLATE CHIP COOKIES

Chorus:

They're made out of sugar and butter and flour;
   You put 'em in the oven about a quarter hour,
But the thing that gives 'em their magic power
   Is the chocolate chips inside.

You can't eat one; you can't eat two;
   Once you start chewing, there's nothing to do
But clean your plate, and eat the crumbs too,
   Then go and find some more.

If you want to make a friend,
   You don't need beauty or money to spend
Give 'em all your love, but be sure you send
   Some chocolate chip cookies, too.

— William Steele

MIXING IT ALL TOGETHER

THE METHOD of combining ingredients for chocolate chip cookies is fairly standard. In the several instances in this book where mixing instructions do vary from the norm, there are reasons for this, and you should follow instructions carefully to get the result the recipe's creator was striving for. Generally speaking, however, the procedure for mixing and baking is as follows.

PANS

First, prepare your baking sheets. This is another one of those points of controversy: to grease or not to grease? Or should you line your pans, and if you line them, should you use aluminum foil or baking parchment? And what kinds of pans anyway? The Orchards chef recommends baking parchment, as greasing pans may cause the cookies to spread too much while baking. The more cakelike cookies, however, may need pans that are lightly greased to avoid real sticking problems. If you do grease, use margarine rather than butter, and be sure to regrease for additional batches.

The kind of pan you use can also affect a cookie's texture. Since shiny pans deflect heat and dark ones retain it, you may find that cookies brown too rapidly and thus burn more easily on dark pans. Similarly, thin metal pans allow the cookies to bake from underneath, and again to burn more readily. Insulated baking sheets seem to produce a softer cookie.

My recommendation is to use heavy, shiny pans with only one raised edge and to line them with parchment paper rather than grease them. This way, after the cookies are allowed to set for a minute or two upon removal from the oven, you can carefully slide paper and cookies right off the pan onto trays or racks without disturbing and breaking the warm cookies. Unfurl a fresh piece of parchment and the pans are ready for the next batch. The kinds and treatment of pans are, like many details in cookie-making, personal preferences based on each cook's experience. Whatever kind you choose, be sure they will fit in your oven with 3 or 4 inches to spare all around to assure proper heat circulation.

ORGANIZING

Next, get your ingredients together. A sure and efficient technique for all cooking and baking is to get everything your recipe calls for out on the counter before you begin. This way you find out *before* you are halfway into the project that you are flat out of baking powder. Put everything you are about to use in one place on the counter, and then move things one by one to another area as you finish with them; you will have an excellent check on whether or not you've included everything the recipe calls for. This is a particularly good method for children to learn, but it works equally well to organize adults.

As was mentioned earlier, many ingredients need to be at room temperature before using: the butter or margarine, to make it soft enough to work with and cream well; the eggs, best to achieve their greatest potential volume; and the chocolate, to prevent it from cooling the batter while baking, thus causing uneven baking.

DRY INGREDIENTS

I like to get the sifting and measuring of dry ingredients out of the way at the start. Usually flour should be sifted before measuring and then resifted with other dry ingredients, such as baking powder and salt, before doing anything else. If you do this onto pieces of waxed paper, you will have a few less bowls

to worry about at clean-up time. Set the dry ingredients aside until they are needed.

PREHEATING THE OVEN

Since your oven needs about 10 or 15 minutes to preheat, this is probably a good moment to turn it to the proper temperature and to arrange the oven racks as you will need them for baking. Testing the oven temperature with a thermometer is a professional and excellent habit. Although cookies are in many ways one of the easiest things to make, they are also one of the easiest to burn, particularly those with butter. It happens so quickly, and so irremediably, especially if your oven overheats. Cookies are less likely to burn in the middle or upper part of the oven, so it's best to use only the center rack, or if you are too impatient to bake only one tray at a time, put one rack one-third of the way up and the other at two-thirds, and then switch the trays from rack to rack about halfway through the baking period.

CREAMING THE BUTTER, SUGAR, AND EGGS

A common mistake in cookie baking is to overmix the dough. Result: tough cookies. Pastry Chef Andrus recommends using a wooden spoon to cream the butter and sugar and to beat in the eggs, and finally to mix in all other ingredients, from flour right to chocolate chips, with one's hands. You are much less apt to overmix when you use this method.

The first step in mixing is usually to cream the butter or margarine. Creaming, as we have seen, means beating the butter or margarine until its texture becomes light and fluffy as air is incorporated into the mixture. While the butter should be somewhat softened for this procedure, if allowed to get too warm it will not absorb the proper amount of air. As the butter changes its texture, gradually add the sugar (or sugars), and continue to cream thoroughly. This step takes a bit of experience to judge: you want a light, fluffy mixture, which requires a good amount of beating, but you must not let the butter get too soft or it will lose its airiness and the cookies will tend to be too runny.

Eggs are usually added one at a time, at this point. They needn't be beaten before adding to the creamed mixture, though it is a good idea to break them into a separate bowl first, just to avoid the problem of getting pieces of broken shell into the batter. As you beat the eggs, you are continuing the process of incorporating air into your batter. The more air, the lighter and tenderer the cookies. When all this is looking as you think it should, you usually are asked to stir in the vanilla extract or other flavoring.

ADDING OTHER INGREDIENTS

Now go back to your dry ingredients, which are measured and set aside ready to be put in. An efficient way of mixing in the dry ingredients is to add a cup or so to the creamed mixture, continuing to beat with a wooden spoon. Add the remaining dry ingredients, and if you wish, get right in and mix the batter with your hands (clean hands, of course, with jewelry removed). This is a particularly good method for children who, first of all, love the whole idea of this procedure, and second, are able to control all that obstinate dough better with their hands than with a spoon, which tends to send globules of batter off in unpredictable directions. The dry ingredients should be blended in completely until no flour shows, but mix *only* until that moment or your cookies will be tough.

The final step is gently to stir in the chocolate chips and nuts (if used). Although as has been mentioned before, chips should not be cold when added, neither should they be soft or the chocolate will begin to mix in with the batter. Similarly, never mix the chips in with an electric mixer. It will chop them up while it mixes them in, and you will lose them in the batter.

CHILLING THE DOUGH

Many people like to refrigerate the dough at this point (in which case, do not preheat the oven, of course, before beginning to put everything together). Chilling the dough seems to blend the flavors together; it also tends to produce a more shapely cookie, one that won't spread all over the pan while baking. I have found that, as with pie dough, the cooler the dough, the flakier the result.

You can also freeze the dough for nine to twelve months. A convenient way to do this is to form the dough into a long roll or cylinder and seal in heavy-duty aluminum freezer foil. When you are ready to bake fresh cookies, thaw the dough, in its packaging, to room temperature. Slice slabs of the desired thickness (usually about ⅜ inch) off the roll and bake as directed in the recipe. When packaging for freezing, be sure to wrap in a little piece of paper with baking directions in case you forget which recipe you used. If you freeze the dough in 1-or 2-dozen servings, you can whip a roll out in emergencies and bake a small batch of cookies to warm the hearts of unexpected guests or salvage the evening meal some night when everything else is quite ho-hum.

FORMING THE COOKIES

Whether or not you take the time to chill the dough, the next step is to form the cookies for baking. Traditionally, chocolate chip cookies fall into the drop cookie category, and most recipes instruct you to drop cookies by teaspoonfuls or tablespoonfuls onto the prepared baking sheets. This is most easily done by using one spoon for scooping up the dough and a second spoon for scraping it off onto the dish. If you like large cookies, use an ice cream scoop with a built-in scraper; a 1 ½-inch scoop will make a 2 ½-inch cookie. Or for a giant 6-inch cookie, use your ⅓-cup dry-measure; be sure to flatten these

cookies some before baking or the centers will never cook through.

An alternative method, even if the recipe doesn't direct it, is to form the dough into balls of whatever size you desire. This is most easily done with chilled dough. You may wish to flatten the balls a bit with the back of a slightly moistened spoon or the bottom of a glass, sometimes dipped in sugar, to allow for more even baking. Cookies made by this method are apt to be of more uniform size and shape than drop cookies.

Be sure to allow enough room between cookies on the baking sheets so that everything doesn't run together. If the dough seems a bit softer than usual, leave extra room. Very generous spacing is needed as well for larger cookies. About 2 inches apart is right for most kinds of 2- to 3-inch cookies.

While one batch of cookies is in the oven baking, leave the additional dough in the refrigerator. This keeps it cool, and also keeps it safer from marauders.

BAKING THE COOKIES

Probably the most critical step in this whole procedure is the next one: baking the cookies. You may think that you've done all the work, now you can clean up the kitchen and relax or move on to other things. But this is not the time for the careless or the amateur. Of all the things you will cook in your lifetime, cookies are one of the most easily burnt, and chocolate chip cookies, especially, are often at their best on the underside rather than the overside of done.

There are many ways to prevent burning. First, as was mentioned above, use an oven thermometer to be sure your oven is at the correct temperature. Eight to ten minutes cooking time doesn't leave much margin for error in oven temperature. Next, always set your timer the moment you close the oven door and the cookies begin baking, and always set it for the shorter amount of time suggested in the recipe. Even so, try to remember to check how everything is going a minute or two before the baking time is up. Third, halfway through baking time switch the baking sheets around in the oven: move the top sheet to the bottom and vice versa, and while you are at it, turn them front to back as well. If you were to move your oven thermometer around in the oven, you would be surprised to find the temperature differences in various parts of the oven. Rotating the baking sheets will help compensate for these differences and assure even browning. Convection ovens bake cookies more quickly, but the heat is still uneven; be sure to turn the sheets in convection ovens as well.

Finally, let your nose as well as your timer be your guide. One of the best parts about baking chocolate chip cookies is the wonderful aroma with which it fills your house—almost reason alone to undertake the project! If you think about that delicious smell as it's happening, you will be able to detect immediately a hint of overbrowned butter or sugar.

When you do remove the baking sheets from the oven, the cookies will be very soft and fragile. They should be allowed to stand on the pans and set for a minute or two before removing to racks to cool (if you can bear to wait). In this short period of time the cookies will continue to bake a bit from their own heat as well as from the heat of the pans. After a moment or two, carefully remove cookies to racks. If you have used baking parchment you can simply slide the whole thing off onto the racks. Otherwise, be sure to use a wide, flexible spatula so that you can get the entire cookie gently onto it. Crisp cookies, especially, are easily broken when this fresh. If thin, crisp cookies stick badly, put them back in the oven *briefly*, melting them just enough to allow them to slip free.

Before placing the next batch of cookies on the sheets that have just been removed from the oven, be sure that the pans are completely cool. Warm pans will cause the cookies to run and spread, and thus possibly to burn. Scrape any crumbs from the first batch off the tray, and regrease or reline the tray, if necessary, before loading on the next batch.

Most of the recipes that follow have an approximate yield noted, but this, of course, depends on how large you make your cookies. It also depends on how much raw dough has been snitched before the things ever make it to the pans!

STORING THE COOKIES

Storage seems to be a rare problem for chocolate chip cookie bakers: the cookies disappear before there's a chance of their getting stale! In fact, some people feel the only way to assure safe storage is to guard them with your life, while others attach to the cookie jar warnings, such as, "Hands Off!" or, more effective still, "You touch, you die!"

Cookies should always be stored in airtight containers. If you use plastic containers, you may wish to put the cookies first into plastic bags to avoid any chance of a petroleumlike smell getting into the cookies from the container. Some cooks prefer lined cookie tins to plastic. If the cookies are particularly soft or sticky, place sheets of waxed paper between layers to prevent them from sticking together, especially in warm weather. Don't store two different flavored cookies in the same container; they will absorb flavors from one another and lose their own distinctive taste.

If cookies get too dry, place them in a plastic bag with a piece of bread or a slice of apple. The cookies will absorb a bit of moisture from the bread and be reinvigorated. Do not use herb or spice bread, for the cookies will absorb the flavors as well as the moisture from the bread. Stale cookies can be refreshed by placing them on baking sheets in a 300°F. oven for a few minutes or by placing them on a paper towel and microwaving for fifteen or twenty seconds.

Almost all cookies freeze extremely well. Although this is one sneaky way to make them a bit harder to get at and thus assure that they last a little longer, many folks love frozen, unthawed cookies, especially for "dunking." For a fresh-baked taste and texture, place frozen cookies in the microwave for fifteen or twenty seconds.

Cookies should be frozen in airtight, rigid contain-ers to keep them from getting broken. If you use a tin of some sort, line it first with a plastic bag to assure airtightness. Place sheets of waxed paper between layers to cushion the cookies. Thaw at room temperature, in the packaging so that they don't become soggy.

For special freezer treats, sandwich your favorite ice cream between two giant-sized cookies, wrap in foil, and freeze.

If you should happen to have a leftover cookie or two (you might just have to *make* this happen), try crumbling it up and adding it to homemade vanilla or chocolate ice cream for your own chocolate chip cookie ice cream.

STRIKING OFF ON YOUR OWN

The above suggestions and advice about cookie making are an attempt at giving you some ideas about the interrelationship between kinds and amounts of ingredients, as well as different mixing and baking techniques, and the final outcome. By trying several recipes and considering what you like best in a chocolate chip cookie, you should be able to use some of this information and develop exactly what you want, be it soft and caky or crisp or chewy, or some combination thereof. As you have seen, there is a basic cookie formula that takes quite kindly to adaptation, and you may be able to develop a recipe so good and workable that you can easily adjust it to various situations.

Begin with the question of whether to use butter, margarine, or shortening, or some combination. Consider the purpose for which you are baking: do you care that butter is more expensive? shortening is likely to provide a longer storage period? Take into account also how much butter/margarine/shortening to use in proportion to other ingredients; the more you use, the chewier, moister, and thinner the cookies will be.

After the butter/margarine/shortening comes the sugar. Not only do you need to settle on an amount that will produce the tenderness and sweetness you desire without being too cloying, but you also have a choice about whether or not to use both brown and white sugar and if you use both, what proportion of each. The Original Toll House recipe uses brown and white sugar in equal proportions, but this ratio can be changed. Some people believe that a tablespoon or two of corn syrup in substitution for some of the sugar will produce a chewier cookie without having to undercook the dough. Honey may have the same effect. Be sure to reduce any other liquid in the dough to compensate for the added liquid in these sweeteners.

Add one or more eggs. Additional egg yolk will produce a cakier cookie.

Vanilla extract is next and can be substituted for or combined with any flavor you think of—almond, peppermint, orange, lemon, and so on.

Flour again offers many possibilities. Although all-purpose flour is most commonly used, some of the amount can be substituted with whole wheat flour for more interesting texture. The more flour you use in proportion to the butter-sugar mixture the thicker and cakier the cookie will be.

The amount of chocolate you use requires a degree of finesse. There are those, of course, who would never believe you could have too much chocolate in a cookie, but you are baking cookies after all, not making candy! In a recent Nestlé survey over half of those questioned thought the ideal cookie should contain 6 to 10 chips, and only 12 percent wanted 20 or more chips in each cookie, but, of course, your only concern is the size of the "chocolate tooth" of those for whom *you* are baking.

For more ideas about varying your recipes, read again the section on ingredients.

Finally, the way you *bake* the cookies will also affect the final result. An oven temperature of about 350°F to 375°F. for about 10 minutes is the most common for chocolate chip cookies, but a harder cookie will result from a longer, slower baking time (say 300°F to 325°F. for 15 or 20 minutes) and a soft, chewy cookie may result from baking at high heat for a shorter period of time (400°F. for 6 to 8 minutes).

Good luck in your endeavors. Remember, chocolate chip cookies are practically impossible to spoil.

THE
COOKIES

TRADITIONAL
CHOCOLATE CHIP
COOKIES

Let's begin with a group of recipes, each of which is quite
similar to the Original Toll House Recipe invented by Mrs.
Wakefield in the early 1930s. The ingredients are all pretty
standard, but each will produce a different texture and taste,
depending on the proportions of those ingredients, the presence
of butter, margarine, or shortening, or even the method of
mixing everything together. We each seem to hold in our
minds some archetype of "The" chocolate chip cookie—is one
of these that model for you?

CHOCOLATE CHIP COOKIES I

1 cup plus 2 tablespoons flour
½ teaspoon baking soda
½ teaspoon salt
½ cup butter
6 tablespoons granulated sugar
6 tablespoons brown sugar, firmly packed

1 egg
½ teaspoon vanilla extract
½ cup chopped nuts (optional)
6 ounces (1 cup) semisweet chocolate chips or semisweet chocolate bar cut into pea-sized pieces

Sift flour before measuring, then resift with baking soda and salt. Set aside.

Cream butter. Add sugars gradually, and continue beating until creamy. Beat in egg and vanilla. Stir in sifted ingredients. Stir in nuts and chocolate chips.

Drop by teaspoonfuls onto greased baking sheets, placing cookies well apart. Bake at 350°F. for about 8 to 10 minutes. *Yield: about 4 dozen*

RICHARD MacDONALD
CHADDS FORD, PENNSYLVANIA

CHOCOLATE CHIP COOKIES II

Softer and chewier than most traditional chocolate chip cookies, these cookies depend for their distinctive texture on adequate beating with an electric beater. Try dipping frozen cookies in hot coffee.

3 cups flour
1 teaspoon baking soda
1 teaspoon salt
1 cup margarine, room temperature
¾ cup granulated sugar

¾ cup light brown sugar, firmly packed
1 teaspoon vanilla
1 teaspoon water
2 eggs
18 ounces (3 cups) semisweet chocolate chips

Sift flour before measuring, then resift with baking soda and salt, and set aside.

Combine margarine, sugars, vanilla, and water in a bowl and beat with an electric mixer about 2 minutes until creamy. Add eggs and beat until fluffy.

Gradually add the sifted ingredients, and beat with electric mixer for about 2 minutes until very well blended.

Stir in chocolate chips.

Drop by heaping teaspoonfuls onto lightly greased baking sheets. Bake on middle oven rack at 350°F. for 10 to 12 minutes. Do not overbake. Remove from oven when lightly browned, slightly crisp on bottom; they may seem slightly undercooked. Cool 1 minute on baking sheet, then remove to paper towels to cool completely.
Yield: about 4 dozen

SUSAN S. GROSSMAN
CANTON, OHIO

CHOCOLATE CHIP COOKIES III

3 cups flour
1 teaspoon baking soda
1 teaspoon salt
1 cup margarine
1⅓ cups granulated sugar

⅔ cup light brown sugar, firmly packed
1½ teaspoons vanilla extract
2 extra large eggs
18 ounces (3 cups) semisweet chocolate chips

Combine without sifting, flour, baking soda, and salt. Set aside.

Cream margarine with sugars until light. Beat in vanilla and eggs until smooth. Beat dry ingredients into creamed mixture, a little at a time. Add chocolate chips, and stir to mix well.

Drop dough by heaping tablespoonfuls onto parchment-lined baking sheets. Bake at 325°F. for 12 minutes, turning sheets end for end about halfway through baking time. Remove from oven and slide parchment off sheets, with cookies still on top. Leave undisturbed until cookies are just barely cool enough to handle. Transfer to racks to cool completely.   *Yield: 3 to 4 dozen*

COLLEEN IERMINI
SANTA CRUZ, CALIFORNIA

CHOCOLATE CHIP COOKIES IV

The success of this recipe is dependent upon rolling up your sleeves and mixing everything with your hands. These are particularly fine dipped in a cold glassful of milk.

4½ cups flour
2 teaspoons baking soda
2 teaspoons salt
1½ cups granulated sugar
1½ cups brown sugar, firmly packed

2 cups shortening
3 eggs
2 teaspoons vanilla extract
12 ounces semisweet chocolate chips
1 cup chopped nuts

In a large mixing bowl, combine flour, baking soda, salt, and sugars. Add shortening, squeezing and kneading dough thoroughly with hands. Add eggs and vanilla, and continue to knead by hand until dough is firm. Add chocolate chips and nuts.

Form 1-inch balls of dough and place about 2 inches apart on ungreased baking sheets. Bake at 375°F. for about 10 to 15 minutes. Remove from oven and allow to cool for about 2 minutes before removing from baking sheets with a spatula to wire racks to cool completely.
Yield: 8 to 9 dozen

RIC TRAEGER
FRESNO, CALIFORNIA

CHOCOLATE CHIP COOKIES V

Developed for the Flying Cloud Inn in New Marlboro, Massachusetts, this traditional cookie can be made soft and chewy or crisp simply by regulating the baking time.

3 cups flour
1 teaspoon baking soda
½ teaspoon salt
1 cup butter, softened
½ cup granulated sugar

1 cup brown sugar, firmly packed
2 teaspoons vanilla extract
2 eggs
9 ounces (1½ cups) semisweet chocolate chips
1 cup chopped walnuts

Sift together flour, baking soda, and salt, and set aside.

In a large bowl, cream together butter, sugars, and vanilla until light. Add eggs one at a time and mix until well blended. Add sifted ingredients, and mix until well combined. Add chocolate chips and nuts and blend well.

Drop by heaping teaspoonfuls 2 inches apart onto well-greased baking sheets. Bake at 350°F. for 8 to 10 minutes, or until lightly browned for a chewy cookie or slightly longer for a crisp one. Let stand on baking sheet for one minute before removing to cooling rack.   *Yield: 6 to 7 dozen*

BEVERLY LANGEVELD
LANESBORO, MASSACHUSETTS

CHOCOLATE CHIP COOKIES VI

For flat, crisp cookies, drop dough by teaspoonfuls onto baking sheets and bake immediately for the longer baking time. If you prefer chewy cookies, however, try refrigerating the dough for a couple of hours and then forming it into balls for baking. Wet hands while working with dough.

1 cup unsalted (sweet) butter
1 teaspoon vanilla extract
1 teaspoon salt
½ cup granulated sugar
1½ cups light brown sugar, firmly packed
2 large eggs

2¼ cups flour
1 teaspoon baking soda
1 teaspoon warm water
24 ounces (4 cups) semisweet chocolate chips
2 cups walnut pieces

Cream butter. Add vanilla, salt, and sugars, and beat until light and fluffy. Add eggs and beat well.

Dissolve baking soda in warm water. Gradually add baking soda mixture and flour to creamed mixture, beating just until all the flour is blended in. Stir in chocolate and walnuts. Do not overmix.

Bake at 375°F. for about 10 minutes, until light brown.   *Yield: 6 dozen*

ALEXIS C. DUCAT
CHERRY HILL, NEW JERSEY

CHOCOLATE CHIP COOKIES VII

2 cups plus 4 tablespoons flour
1 teaspoon baking soda
1 teaspoon salt
1 cup granulated sugar
½ cup brown sugar, firmly packed
2 eggs

1 teaspoon vanilla extract
1 cup butter or margarine, softened till almost melted
12 ounces (2 cups) semisweet chocolate chips
2 cups coarsely chopped walnuts (optional)

Sift flour, with baking soda and salt. Add sugars, eggs, vanilla, and butter, and beat with a wooden spoon until smooth and well combined. Stir in chocolate chips and nuts.

Drop by teaspoonfuls onto ungreased baking sheets, placing cookies about 2 inches apart. Bake at 375°F. for 10 to 12 minutes, or until golden. Remove to wire racks to cool. *Yield: 8 dozen*

MONA B. SPENCER
VANCOUVER, WASHINGTON

The remainder of the recipes in this section are all "traditional" in that each is a golden cookie filled with chocolate chips of some sort. But with varying degrees of adventuresomeness, each has a special fillip or two that takes it out of the ordinary—from a dash of almond or coconut flavoring, through experiments with corn syrup in place of sugar or oil in place of butter, to the use of milk chocolate or butterscotch chips, or combinations of chocolates, or even other kinds of candy and dried fruit.

CHOCOLATE CHIP COOKIES WITH OIL

When formed and baked properly these cookies from an old family recipe are soft and chewy with a lovely golden tint to them. Though dough may be chilled before baking, allow it to return to room temperature before putting cookies in oven. These cookies do not turn out as well when cooked in a convection oven.

3 cups flour
1 teaspoon baking soda
½ teaspoon salt
½ cup granulated sugar
1 cup brown sugar
1 cup vegetable oil (do not substitute butter, margarine or shortening)

2 eggs
1 teaspoon vanilla extract
12 ounces (2 cups) semisweet chocolate chips
¾ cup chopped walnut pieces (optional)

Sift together the flour, baking soda, and salt; set aside.

Combine both the sugars and oil thoroughly using an electric mixer. Add eggs and vanilla, and beat well. Add sifted ingredients to creamed mixture, 1 cup at a time, beating dough well after each addition of flour. Stir in chocolate chips and nuts.

Place heaping teaspoonfuls on ungreased baking sheets. Bake at 350°F. for 7 to 8 minutes.
Yield: about 4 dozen

THERESA R. KENNEDY
MIDDLEPORT, OHIO

GRANDMA'S CHOCOLATE CHIP COOKIES WITH OIL

A small amount of vegetable oil makes these nice-looking cookies especially crispy. The recipe is an adaptation of one given by a radio cook of the 1940s.

1 cup plus 2 tablespoons flour
½ teaspoon baking soda
¼ teaspoon salt
¼ cup butter
¼ cup margarine
6 tablespoons granulated sugar

6 tablespoons brown sugar
1 egg
½ teaspoon vanilla extract
1 tablespoon corn oil
1 cup semisweet chocolate chips
½ cup chopped walnuts

Sift together flour, baking soda, and salt, and set aside.

Cream together butter, margarine, and sugars until fluffy. Add egg, vanilla, and corn oil. Add sifted ingredients to creamed mixture, blending well. Stir in chocolate chips and nuts.

Drop by teaspoonfuls onto ungreased baking sheets. Bake at 375°F. for 8 to 10 minutes. Allow cookies to remain on baking sheets about 2 minutes before removing to racks with metal spatula to cool. *Yield: about 4 dozen*

THELMA LAPREY
PAWTUCKET, RHODE ISLAND

NUTTY CHOCOLATE CHIP COOKIES

If you don't like chunks of nuts in your cookies, here is a compromise: grind the nuts finely to get the flavor of nuts without the pieces. An extra ¼ cup flour will make these cookies chewier.

2¼ cups flour
1 teaspoon baking soda
1 teaspoon salt
1 cup margarine
¾ cup sugar

2 eggs
¾ teaspoon vanilla extract
¼ teaspoon almond extract
1 cup semisweet chocolate chips
½ cup (or less) finely ground pecans (optional)

Sift together the flour, soda, and salt three times, and set aside.

Cream together the margarine, sugar, eggs, and vanilla and almond extracts. Stir sifted ingredients into creamed mixture, along with pecans if used.

Drop by teaspoonfuls onto greased baking sheets. Bake at 350°F. for 10 minutes. *Yield: 2 to 3 dozen*

PAMELA McCARTNEY
CHAMPAIGN, ILLINOIS

BIG BATCH CHIP COOKIES

This excellent, large, soft cookie is an old family recipe, rich in flavor, with more than usually generous amounts of butter and vanilla.

4 cups flour
1½ teaspoons baking soda
1¼ teaspoons salt
1½ cups butter, softened
1½ cups granulated sugar
¾ cup dark brown sugar, firmly packed

3 large eggs
3 teaspoons vanilla extract
1 teaspoon almond extract (optional)
12 ounces (2 cups) semisweet chocolate chips
½ cup chopped walnuts or pecans (optional)
½ cup coconut (optional)

Sift together flour, baking soda, and salt; set aside.

Cream butter, sugars, eggs, and vanilla and almond extracts. Stir in sifted ingredients. Gently stir in chocolate chips, nuts, and coconut.

Drop by rounded tablespoons onto greased baking sheets. Bake at 375°F. for 10 minutes, or until edges of cookies turn golden. Do not overbake; cookies will continue baking after being removed from oven. Allow to set for a few minutes on trays before gently removing to racks to cool.   *Yield: 4 to 5 dozen*

ANGELINE BIRDSALL
CORNING, NEW YORK

THREE-CHIP CHOCOLATE CHIP COOKIES

The appearance and taste of this wonderful cookie with its variety of imported chocolates make up for its rather high price tag. Bake just before your family is due home or before guests are coming—a house filled with that tantalizing aroma is probably half the pleasure of chocolate chip cookies.

2½ cups flour
1 teaspoon baking soda
½ teaspoon salt
½ cup butter or margarine, softened
½ cup shortening
½ cup granulated sugar
1 cup light brown sugar, firmly packed
2 eggs
2 tablespoons light corn syrup

2 tablespoons water
2 teaspoons vanilla extract
12 ounces (2 cups) semisweet chocolate chips
8-ounce package Fred's White Chocolate Chips
2 3-½-ounce packages Lindt Chocoletti Swiss Milk Chocolate
2 3-ounce Lindt Milk Chocolate Bars, broken into squares

Combine flour, baking soda, and salt, and set aside.

Cream together butter or margarine, shortening, sugars, eggs, corn syrup, water, and vanilla, and beat well. Add dry ingredients to creamed mixture, and beat well. With a large wooden spoon, gently stir in all chocolate pieces.

Chill dough at least one hour.

With moistened hands, roll dough into walnut-sized pieces, and place on baking sheets lined with aluminum foil. (Do not grease foil.) Bake at 375°F. for 10 to 12 minutes until *very* lightly browned. Cool for about 2 minutes before removing from pans. *Yield: 3 to 4 dozen*

BARBARA LERCH
NORTHBROOK, ILLINOIS

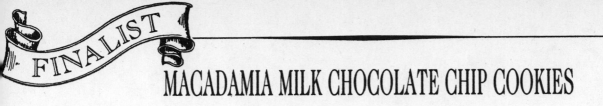
MACADAMIA MILK CHOCOLATE CHIP COOKIES

Very large chips for very large cookies.

2¼ cups flour
1 teaspoon baking soda
½ teaspoon salt
1 cup margarine
¾ cup sugar
¾ cup brown sugar, firmly packed

2 eggs
1½ teaspoons vanilla extract
2 cups large milk chocolate chips (such as Guittard)
¾ cup chopped macadamia nuts
½ cup flaked coconut

Sift together flour, baking soda, and salt, and set aside.

Cream margarine. Gradually add sugars, and beat until fluffy. Add eggs one at a time, mixing well after each addition. Stir in vanilla. Add sifted ingredients, and beat until well blended.

Stir in milk chocolate chips, macadamia nuts, and coconut.

Drop by ¼ cupfuls onto ungreased baking sheets, placing cookies 3 inches apart. Bake at 375°F. for 16 to 19 minutes, until golden. *Yield: 2 dozen*

JAN DEERING
WICHITA, KANSAS

WHITE CHOCOLATE-MACADAMIA NUT CHIPPERS

*For a special birthday treat make 6-inch cookies and serve warm topped with vanilla ice cream.
To cut costs a bit, substitute 1 cup semisweet chocolate chips for 1 cup of the white chocolate
chips, and use almonds instead of macadamia nuts.
The optional coconut was the special invention of the recipe creator's two-year-old son, who
tossed in a handful when his mother wasn't looking.*

2 cups flour
1 teaspoon baking soda
½ teaspoon salt
1 cup butter or margarine, softened
¾ cup granulated sugar
¾ cup brown sugar, firmly packed

1 egg
1 teaspoon vanilla extract
12 ounces (2 cups) white chocolate chips, or bulk
   white chocolate cut into ¼-inch chunks
½ cup macadamia nuts, coarsely chopped
½ cup coconut (optional)

Mix flour, baking soda, and salt, and set aside.

Beat butter, sugars, and egg until fluffy. Stir in the dry ingredients. Blend in the vanilla. Gently stir in the chocolate, nuts, and coconut.

Drop by tablespoonfuls onto ungreased baking sheets, placing cookies a few inches apart. Bake at 375°F. for 8 to 10 minutes until golden brown. Cool slightly, and remove to wire racks to cool completely.   *Yield: 2½ dozen*

DANITA YANNIELLO
BURBANK, CALIFORNIA

DAD'S FAVORITE MILK CHOCOLATE CHIP COOKIES

6 cups flour
1½ teaspoons baking soda
1½ teaspoons salt
2 cups butter
1 cup granulated sugar
2½ cups brown sugar, firmly packed

3 eggs
2 tablespoons vanilla extract
3 cups semisweet chocolate chips
3 cups milk chocolate chips
2 cups chopped pecans (or 1 cup pecans/1 cup walnuts)

Sift together flour, baking soda, and salt, and set aside.

Combine the butter, sugars, eggs, and vanilla, and cream very well. Add the sifted ingredients to the creamed mixture, and mix well. Stir in chocolate chips and nuts.

Shape into balls. Bake at 350°F. for 7 to 9 minutes. *Do not overbake*; sides should be slightly browned, but centers will look gooey. *Yield: about 6 dozen*

KAREN KLOOZ HUNTER
HAY SPRINGS, NEBRASKA

CAKEY CHOCOLATE CHIP COOKIES

A soft, cakelike cookie, delightful with afternoon tea or hot chocolate.
To make the chocolate pieces for this cookie, first chill chocolate bars. Working with only one bar of chocolate at a time, break off pieces of chocolate into dry bowl of food processor. With metal blade, pulsate machine until chocolate is of desired size; do not overprocess. Size of pieces will vary.

3¼ cups flour
1 teaspoon baking soda
½ teaspoon salt
1 cup unsalted (sweet) butter, room temperature
1¼ cups sugar

3 eggs
1 cup milk
1 teaspoon vanilla extract
3 4-ounce bars semisweet chocolate, broken into
   small pieces

Sift together flour, baking soda, and salt; set aside.

Cream butter and sugar. Add eggs one at a time, beating well after each addition. Gradually add sifted ingredients to creamed mixture alternately with milk. Add vanilla. Beat with electric mixer until well mixed, scraping bowl occasionally with rubber spatula. Stir in chocolate pieces by hand.

Drop by heaping tablespoonfuls onto greased baking sheets, placing cookies about 2 inches apart. If desired, press each cookie into a neat circle with a moistened fork. Bake on middle oven rack at 375°F. for 12 to 14 minutes, until edges are lightly browned. Cool thoroughly on wire racks before storing in a covered container. *Yield: 3 dozen*

MARY A. CHRISTMANN
LOS ALTOS, CALIFORNIA

MELT-IN-YOUR-MOUTH TRIPLE CHOCOLATE CHIP COOKIES

These cookies are for serious chocolate lovers who like their cookies very sweet. Be sure to sift the flour before measuring; too much flour will make the cookies tough.

1 cup flour
½ teaspoon baking soda
¼ teaspoon salt
½ cup unsalted (sweet) butter, slightly softened
¼ cup granulated sugar
½ cup dark brown sugar, firmly packed
1 egg

1 teaspoon vanilla extract
½ cup pecans, coarsely chopped
¾ cup semisweet chocolate chips
¾ cup milk chocolate chips
4 ounces white chocolate, cut in tiny cubes

Sift the flour before measuring, then resift with baking soda and salt, and set aside.

Cream butter in a large mixing bowl. Add sugars and beat until smooth and fluffy. Add egg and beat until smooth. Add vanilla; beat until well blended.

Using a wooden spoon, stir in sifted ingredients until blended. Stir in nuts and all chocolate pieces.

Drop by teaspoonfuls onto greased baking sheets, using about 1 tablespoon dough for each cookie and spacing them about 2 inches apart.

Bake on center rack of oven at 375°F. for about 10 minutes, or until browned around edges and nearly set, but still soft to the touch in the center. Using metal spatula, carefully transfer cookies to racks to cool completely.

For additional batches, be sure baking sheets are cool, clean off any crumbs, and grease sheets again.

Cookies store well for up to one week at room temperature in an airtight container.   *Yield: about 4 dozen*

Marcella A. Scalf
San Antonio, Texas

MILK CHOCOLATE CHIP COOKIES

To assure even baking, rotate cookie sheets halfway through baking period, turning sheets front to back and exchanging sheets from top to bottom oven racks. These cookies freeze especially well.

3 cups flour
1 teaspoon baking soda
1 teaspoon salt
1 cup margarine
1⅓ cups granulated sugar
⅔ cup brown sugar

1½ teaspoons vanilla
2 extra large eggs
1 2-ounce milk chocolate bar, grated
12 ounces (2 cups) semisweet chocolate chips
1 cup chopped nuts: walnuts, cashews, macadamias, or pecans

Mix without sifting flour, baking soda, and salt. Set aside.

Cream margarine with sugars until light. Beat in vanilla and eggs until smooth. Add grated chocolate bar.

Beat dry ingredients into creamed mixture.

Add the chocolate chips and nuts, and stir to mix thoroughly.

Drop onto ungreased baking sheets, one heaping tablespoonful at a time. Bake at 325°F. for about 12 minutes.   *Yield: 5 dozen*

KELLY LUCARELLI
BEAVERTON, OREGON

CRÈME DE MENTHE CHOCOLATE CHUNK COOKIES

If you are in a hurry, spread dough over bottom of 9 x 11-inch baking pan, and bake at 350°F. for 20 to 25 minutes. When cool, cut into squares.

2 cups flour
1 teaspoon baking soda
¼ to ½ teaspoon salt
1 cup butter, softened
1 cup granulated sugar
½ cup brown sugar, firmly packed
2 teaspoons vanilla extract

2 eggs
8 ounces Swiss semisweet chocolate, cut into
  ½-inch chunks
1¼ cups chopped almonds (optional)
3 dozen pieces crème de menthe candy, cut into
  quarters

Combine flour, baking soda, and salt, and set aside.

Beat butter, sugars, vanilla, and eggs until light and fluffy. Blend in dry ingredients. Stir in chocolate chunks, almonds, and crème de menthe candy. Chill for 1 hour.

Remove from refrigerator and allow to stand for 10 minutes. Drop by heaping tablespoonfuls onto ungreased baking sheets, placing cookies about 2 inches apart. Bake at 350°F. for 12 to 15 minutes, or until lightly browned. Do not overbake. Cook 2 minutes; remove from sheet and cool upside down on racks. *Yield: 3½ dozen*

MARY CRAMER
NORTH ADAMS, MASSACHUSETTS

CHOCOLATE & PEANUT BUTTER CHIP COOKIES

Be sure both chocolate and peanut butter chips are cool when you mix them into the batter; soft chips will lose their shape and begin to blend into the batter. For a soft cookie, avoid overbaking.

2¾ cups flour
1 teaspoon baking soda
½ cup butter, softened
½ cup shortening
½ cup granulated sugar
1 cup light brown sugar, firmly packed

3 eggs
1½ teaspoons vanilla extract
1½ cups chopped walnuts
12 ounces (2 cups) semisweet chocolate chips
12 ounces (2 cups) peanut butter chips

Combine flour and baking soda; set aside.

With electric mixer, cream butter and shortening together. Gradually add sugars. Add eggs one at a time, beating well after each addition. Add vanilla.

Stir in dry ingredients and mix well. Add walnuts and chocolate and peanut butter chips. Mix well with hands; mixture will be stiff.

Drop by rounded tablespoonfuls onto well-greased baking sheets. Refrigerate unused dough while batches are baking. Bake at 325°F. for 10 to 12 minutes, or until light brown. Cookies will continue to bake when removed from oven. *Yield: 4 dozen*

MIKE COLEY
FORT LAUDERDALE, FLORIDA
AND
DEBORAH ANN COLEY-FLOYD
BILOXI, MISSISSIPPI

MINTY-NUT & RAISIN CHOCOLATE CHIP COOKIES

1¼ cups all-purpose flour
½ teaspoon baking soda
½ teaspoon salt
½ cup butter or margarine
⅓ cup granulated sugar
⅓ cup brown sugar, firmly packed

1 egg
½ teaspoon vanilla extract
⅔ cup nuts, coarsely chopped (preferably pecans)
⅔ cup mint-chocolate morsels
½ cup raisins

Sift together flour, salt, and baking soda, and set aside.

Cream butter and sugars well in a medium mixing bowl. Add egg and vanilla, and beat well.

Add sifted ingredients to butter mixture. Gently mix in nuts, mint-chocolate morsels, and raisins.

Bake at 350°F. for 10 minutes. *Yield: 4½ dozen*

EDWARD S. TOOMER
BILOXI, MISSISSIPPI

APRICOT CHOCOLATE CHIP COOKIES

An old-fashioned recipe for people who enjoy cookies with nice texture that are not overly sweet. The larger the apricot slices, the chewier the cookie.

1½ cups flour
¼ teaspoon baking soda
¼ teaspoon salt
⅓ cup plus 3 tablespoons margarine
1 cup brown sugar, firmly packed

1 egg, beaten
1 teaspoon vanilla extract
6 ounces dried apricots
½ cup chopped walnuts
6 ounces (1 cup) semisweet chocolate chips

Sift together flour, baking soda, and salt, and set aside.

Cream margarine. Add sugar, and mix thoroughly. Add egg and vanilla; blend well. Add sifted ingredients.

Cut apricots into pieces with scissors, and add to batter along with nuts and chocolate chips.

Drop by teaspoonfuls onto greased baking sheets. Bake at 350°F. for about 10 minutes. Allow to cool partially before removing from baking sheets.   *Yield: 3½ dozen*

PAT KITE
NEWARK, CALIFORNIA

GOLDEN RAISIN CHOCOLATE CHIP COOKIES

*The success of this cookie depends on using golden raisins, which
impart chewiness, moistness, and a slightly tart flavor.*

2¼ cups flour
1 teaspoon baking soda
1 teaspoon salt
1 cup butter, softened
¾ cup granulated sugar

¾ cup brown sugar, firmly packed
1 teaspoon vanilla
2 eggs
12 ounces (2 cups) semisweet chocolate chips
1½ cups golden raisins

Combine flour, baking soda, and salt; set aside.
In a large bowl, combine butter, sugars, and
vanilla, and beat until creamy. Beat in eggs.
Gradually stir in dry ingredients, mixing well.
Stir in chocolate chips and raisins.

Drop by rounded tablespoonfuls onto ungreased
baking sheets. Bake 10 to 13 minutes at 375°F
Yield: 2½ dozen

DIANE BUNTROCK
GIBSONIA, PENNSYLVANIA

CUISINE D'OR CHOCOLATE CHUNK COOKIES

Crisp outsides and chewy centers, are often achieved by undercooking. In this recipe a small amount of corn syrup is substituted for some of the granulated sugar, for a chewy texture without being soft or undercooked. Store cookies in the refrigerator.

2 ⅛ cups flour
¾ teaspoon baking soda
pinch salt
1 cup unsalted butter, slightly cooler than room temperature
1¾ cups minus 1½ tablespoons brown sugar, firmly packed
1½ tablespoons corn syrup

2 large eggs, room temperature, lightly beaten
2 teaspoons vanilla extract
⅛ teaspoon almond extract
8 ounces Swiss milk chocolate, cut into small chunks
8 ounces Swiss semisweet chocolate, cut into small chunks

Mix flour with soda and salt, and set aside.

With an electric mixer, cream the butter until softened. Add sugar; cream until light and fluffy. Blend in the corn syrup, scraping down the bowl often.

Blend in the lightly beaten eggs, and vanilla and almond extracts. If the mixture seems curdled or unhomogenous, add a bit of the flour mixture to bind it.

Stir dry ingredients into creamed mixture, scraping down sides of bowl occasionally. Stir in chocolate pieces gently by hand.

Chill batter 20 minutes. Line a baking sheet with parchment paper.

Drop by rounded teaspoonfuls onto parchment-lined baking sheets. Flatten cookies very slightly. Bake at 350°F. for 12 minutes, or until cookies are lightly golden brown. Cool 1 minute on pans, then remove to cooking rack. Store in the refrigerator to preserve flavors. *Yield: 4 dozen*

MARCY GOLDMAN-POSLUNS
MONTREAL, QUEBEC

JOYOUS CHOCOLATE CHIP COOKIES

Another cookie whose crisp, firm outside and soft, chewy inside is attained by the use of corn syrup in place of some of the sugar normally called for.

3 cups flour
1 teaspoon baking soda
1 teaspoon salt
½ cup butter
¼ cup shortening
½ cup granulated sugar
1 cup brown sugar, firmly packed

1 teaspoon vanilla extract
2 eggs
1 tablespoon milk
3 tablespoons dark corn syrup
12 ounces (2 cups) semisweet chocolate chips
½ cup pecans, broken

Sift together flour, baking soda, and salt, and set aside.

Cream butter and shortening together. Gradually add sugars, and cream thoroughly.

Mix together vanilla, eggs, milk, and corn syrup, and add to creamed mixture, beating until blended. Gradually add dry ingredients, mixing well. Add chocolate chips and nuts.

Form into small balls, or drop by teaspoonfuls onto greased baking sheets. Bake at 350°F. for 7 to 10 minutes. Cookies are done when golden brown, with slightly darker edges. When touched with a fingertip, a slight dimple should remain though cookie does not collapse. *Yield: about 4 dozen*

ROBIN JOY MINNICK
DONELSON, TENNESSEE

BLACK WALNUT CHOCOLATE CHIP COOKIES

Black walnuts give this cookie its distinctive flavor. If they are not available in your area, they can be mail-ordered from Sunnyland Farms, Inc., Willson Road at Pecan City, P. O. Box 8200, Albany, GA 31706-8200.

3 cups flour
1¼ teaspoons baking soda
1 teaspoon baking powder
1 cup granulated sugar
1 cup brown sugar, firmly packed
1 cup shortening

2 eggs
2 teaspoons vanilla extract
½ cup water
2 tablespoons powdered buttermilk
18 ounces (3 cups) semisweet chocolate chips
1 cup chopped black walnuts

Sift together flour, baking soda, and baking powder, and set aside.

Cream sugars and shortening until smooth. Beat in eggs and vanilla.

Mix powdered buttermilk with water until smooth. Add to creamed mixture. Stir in sifted ingredients until well blended. Add chocolate chips and nuts, stirring until they are evenly mixed in.

Drop by tablespoonfuls onto greased baking sheets. Bake at 400°F. for 10 to 12 minutes. *Yield: 4 dozen*

LINDA JOHNSON
MCKEESPORT, PENNSYLVANIA

TRADITIONAL
CHOCOLATE CHIP
COOKIES PLUS

When plain chocolate chip cookies seem just not quite enough,
when you are looking for a bit more or, perhaps, a lot less,
crunch, when spiciness or fruitiness would hit the spot, or
when a honey, molasses, or maple syrup enthusiast is close at
hand, leaf through the following group of recipes for
something sure to please.

CRISP RICE CHOCOLATE CHIP COOKIES

1¾ cups flour
1 teaspoon baking soda
½ teaspoon salt
1 cup butter or margarine, softened
¾ cup granulated sugar

¾ cup brown sugar, firmly packed
2 eggs
1 teaspoon vanilla extract
2 cups crisp rice cereal
6 ounces (1 cup) semisweet chocolate chips

Mix together flour, baking soda, and salt, and set aside.

Combine butter and sugars, and beat until well blended. Add eggs and vanilla, and beat well. Add dry ingredients, mixing until combined. Stir in cereal and chocolate chips.

Drop by tablespoonfuls onto greased baking sheets. Bake at 350°F. for about 10 minutes, or until lightly browned. Cool on trays for about 1 minute before removing to cooling racks.
Yield: about 3 dozen

MARIE H. JACKSON
LEXINGTON, KENTUCKY

POTATO CHIP-CHOCOLATE CHIP COOKIES

Try varying this recipe by substituting peanut butter chips for some or all of the chocolate chips, or using rum or lemon extract in addition to the vanilla extract.

2 cups flour
1 teaspoon baking soda
1 cup butter or margarine
1 cup granulated sugar
1 cup light brown sugar, firmly packed

2 eggs
1 teaspoon vanilla extract
2 cups potato chips, coarsely crushed
6 ounces (1 cup) semisweet chocolate chips
1 cup chopped nuts (optional)

Mix together the flour and baking soda, and set aside.

Cream butter, sugars, and eggs until smooth and well blended. Stir in vanilla. Stir in dry ingredients, and mix well. Gently add potato chips and chocolate chips, then nuts, and mix well to distribute everything evenly.

Drop by teaspoonfuls onto ungreased baking sheets. Bake at 350°F. for 10 to 12 minutes. *Yield: 9 dozen*

DERENE WILSON
CLEARLAKE, CALIFORNIA

SPICY CHOCOLATE CHIP COOKIES

Keep this richly spiced cookie tightly covered to preserve its moistness.

2 cups all-purpose flour
2 cups whole wheat flour
4 teaspoons cinnamon
1 teaspoon baking soda
1 teaspoon salt
½ teaspoon ginger
½ teaspoon cloves
2 cups brown sugar
½ cup honey (optional)

1½ cups shortening
4 eggs
1 teaspoon vanilla extract
1 cup water
4 cups rolled oats
12 ounces (2 cups) or more semisweet chocolate chips
1 cup nuts (optional)

Sift together flours, cinnamon, baking soda, salt, ginger, and cloves, and set aside.

Cream together sugar, honey, and shortening. Add eggs and vanilla. Add sifted ingredients to creamed mixture. Add water and rolled oats, and mix well. Gently stir in chocolate chips and nuts.

Drop by teaspoonfuls onto greased baking sheets. Bake at 350°F. for 12 to 15 minutes. *Yield: 3 dozen*

LINDA LEATHERMAN
MULVANE, KANSAS

SPICY CHOCOLATE CHIP PUMPKIN COOKIES

Steam or bake fresh pumpkin, purée, and freeze in plastic bags in 1-cup portions that can be readily thawed for use in this recipe for up to one year. Canned pumpkin purée may be substituted for fresh.

2 cups flour
4 teaspoons baking powder
1 tablespoon cinnamon
½ teaspoon nutmeg
¼ teaspoon ginger
1 teaspoon salt

½ cup shortening
1 cup sugar
2 large eggs, beaten
1 cup pumpkin purée
6 ounces (1 cup) semisweet chocolate chips

Sift together flour, baking powder, cinnamon, nutmeg, ginger, and salt, and set aside.

Cream shortening. Gradually add sugar. Add beaten eggs and pumpkin, and mix well. Blend in sifted ingredients until well mixed. Add chocolate chips.

Drop by teaspoonfuls onto greased baking sheets. Bake at 350°F. on top rack of oven for 15 minutes. *Yield: 5 to 6 dozen*

CONNIE CWYNAR
CAPE CORAL, FLORIDA

SPICY FROSTBITE CHOCOLATE CHIP COOKIES

These are a good choice when you need cookies to pack up and mail. The teenager who invented this recipe is now away at college and likes to receive boxes of her creation from home.

2 cups flour
1 teaspoon baking soda
2 teaspoons cinnamon, divided
1 teaspoon ground ginger
¼ teaspoon salt
1 cup butter

1½ cups brown sugar, firmly packed
1 egg
1½ teaspoons vanilla extract
12 ounces (2 cups) semisweet chocolate chips
1 cup chopped pecans or walnuts
2 cups confectioners' sugar

Sift together flour, baking soda, 1½ teaspoons cinnamon, ginger, and salt. Set aside.

Cream butter. Add brown sugar, egg, and vanilla, and beat well. Add sifted ingredients to butter mixture. Gently stir in chocolate and nuts.

Refrigerate overnight or until firm. Form balls using 1 tablespoon of dough.

Mix remaining ½ teaspoon cinnamon with confectioners' sugar. Roll balls in sugar mixture. Place about 2 inches apart on ungreased baking sheets. Bake at 350°F. for 15 minutes. *Yield: about 3 dozen*

SHERLYN B. MORRISSETTE
LYNDONVILLE, VERMONT

CALIFORNIA CHOCOLATE CHIP COOKIES

A not-too-sweet cookie with the sunshine taste of fresh oranges.

3 cups flour
1 teaspoon baking soda
1 teaspoon salt
⅔ cup ground walnuts
1 cup margarine, softened
¾ cup granulated sugar
1 cup dark brown sugar, firmly packed

2 teaspoons vanilla extract
2 large eggs
1 tablespoon orange juice
1½ tablespoons finely chopped orange zest
18 ounces (3 cups) semisweet chocolate chips
1½ cups coarsely chopped walnuts

Sift together flour, baking soda, and salt. Mix in ground walnuts and set aside.

In large mixing bowl, cream margarine with sugars until light and fluffy. Add vanilla, eggs, orange juice, and orange zest, and beat until smooth. Add sifted ingredients until completely blended. Add chocolate chips and walnuts, and stir well to distribute evenly.

Form dough into balls a bit larger than walnuts, or drop by tablespoonfuls onto parchment-lined baking sheets. Bake at 350°F. for about 10 minutes, just until a very light golden color. With a spatula, transfer cookies to racks to cool.   *Yield: 4½ dozen*

LIBIA FOGLESONG
SAN BRUNO, CALIFORNIA

ORANGE CHOCOLATE CHIP COOKIES

Tangy orange and rich chocolate combine for a refreshing taste of warm, exotic places. Be sure to chill dough and baking sheets, or cookies will spread. Do not crowd on sheets, and rotate sheets in oven part way through baking period.

2¼ cups flour
1 teaspoon salt
1 cup butter, softened
¾ cup light brown sugar, firmly packed
½ cup granulated sugar
¼ cup honey
2 eggs, room temperature, beaten

1 teaspoon baking soda dissolved in 1 teaspoon hot water
1 tablespoon finely grated fresh orange peel
12 ounces (2 cups) semisweet chocolate minichips
1 teaspoon vanilla extract
1 cup chopped nuts (optional)

Sift flour before measuring, then resift with salt; set aside.

With an electric mixer, cream butter and sugars in a large bowl until light, fluffy, and pale yellow. Blend in honey. Add beaten eggs. Continue to beat on medium speed for about 2 minutes.

Add dissolved baking soda. Gradually add sifted ingredients, beating well after each addition. Stir in orange peel, chocolate chips, vanilla, and nuts. Chill dough for 1 hour.

Drop by rounded teaspoonfuls onto *chilled* and lightly greased baking sheets. Flatten cookies slightly with the bottom of a glass dipped lightly in granulated sugar to prevent sticking. Bake 10 to 12 minutes, or until lightly browned. Cool cookies on wire racks.   *Yield: about 8 dozen*

NANCY G. MEANS
MOLINE, ILLINOIS

APRICOT CHOCOLATE CHIP COOKIES

The dried apricots for this recipe should be plump, moist, and tender. If you are stuck with brown, shriveled, and brittle ones, however, be sure to simmer them in water until they have softened before using. Save the cooking water and add it to juice, gelatin, sliced fruit, and so on. For a soft, chewy cookie, bake for the shorter amount of time; if you prefer a crisp, hard cookie for "dunking," bake longer.

1½ cups flour
1¼ teaspoons baking powder
¼ cup dried apricots
⅓ cup butter, softened

⅔ cup sugar
1 egg
6 tablespoons apricot preserves
6 ounces (1 cup) semisweet chocolate chips

Sift the flour and baking powder together, and set aside.

Chop or snip the dried apricots into pieces slightly smaller than the chips. Cover them with boiling water, and set aside.

Blend butter and sugar together until light and creamy. Add egg and apricot preserves and continue to beat until well blended. Pieces of apricot will remain visible.

Stir sifted ingredients into creamed mixture until well blended. Fold in chocolate chips.

Drain water from apricot bits and fold them into batter.

Drop batter by teaspoonfuls onto ungreased baking sheets, placing cookies about 2 inches apart. Bake at 375°F. for 8 to 12 minutes, or until edges are slightly brown. *Yield: 3 dozen*

GINA M. GLICK
CARROLLTON, TEXAS

GRANDMA MATTHEWS' MOLASSES CHOCOLATE CHIP COOKIES

This family recipe is well over 100 years old. Grandma Matthews, who firmly believed in the benefits of blackstrap molasses, kept a jug of it on the table and used quantities of it in all her baking.

2½ cups flour, sifted
1 teaspoon baking powder
½ teaspoon salt
¾ cup butter
¾ cup granulated sugar
¾ cup brown sugar, firmly packed

1 egg, well beaten
¼ cup molasses
1 teaspoon vanilla extract
3 tablespoons milk
1 cup semisweet chocolate chips
½ cup chopped walnuts

Sift flour with baking powder and salt, and set aside.

Cream butter with sugars until mixture is light and fluffy. Add egg and molasses.

Stir vanilla into milk, and add to butter mixture alternately with sifted ingredients. Gently stir in chocolate chips and nuts.

Drop by teaspoonfuls onto ungreased baking sheets. Bake at 325°F. for 10 to 12 minutes. *Yield: 4 dozen*

EDITH STACEY
FITCHBURG, MASSACHUSETTS

APPLE ORCHARD CHOCOLATE CHIPPERS

Apple butter in these cookies adds a delicious spiciness and also helps keep them moist.

½ cup butter or margarine
½ cup granulated sugar
¼ cup brown sugar, firmly packed
1 egg
1 teaspoon vanilla extract
¼ cup apple butter

1½ to 2 cups unbleached flour
½ teaspoon baking soda
½ teaspoon salt
6 ounces (1 cup) semisweet chocolate chips
1 apple, cored and shredded
½ cup nuts (optional)

In a large mixing bowl, cream butter, sugars, egg, and vanilla until light and fluffy. Add apple butter, and mix well.

Add 1 cup flour, baking soda, and salt, and mix until well blended. Gradually add remaining flour just until dough is no longer wet and sticky.

Stir in chocolate chips, shredded apple, and nuts.

Drop dough by teaspoonfuls onto lightly greased baking sheets, placing cookies about 2 inches apart. Bake at 350°F. for 12 to 15 minutes. Cool on rack.   *Yield: 3 to 4 dozen*

SHIRLEY DESANTIS
EAST WINDSOR, NEW JERSEY

HONEY CHOCOLATE CHIP COOKIES

Because honey retains and absorbs moisture, it is a great substitute for sugar when you want cookies that will not dry out. When substituting honey for sugar in other recipes, use three quarters the amount of honey as the amount listed for sugar, and reduce the amount of other liquid in the recipe by ¼ cup for each cup of honey. This recipe was first published by the Nova Scotia Department of Agriculture and Marketing in a small booklet called Honey Recipes.

1 cup flour
1 teaspoon baking powder
¼ teaspoon salt
½ cup shortening
½ cup honey

1 small egg
½ teaspoon vanilla extract
½ cup semisweet chocolate chips
¼ cup nut meats, chopped

Sift flour before measuring, then resift twice with the baking powder and salt. Set aside.

Cream shortening and honey very well until light and fluffy. Add egg and beat well. Add sifted ingredients to shortening mixture. Add vanilla, and blend well. Fold in chocolate chips and nuts. Chill.

Drop by teaspoonfuls onto greased baking sheets. Bake at 375°F. for 12 minutes. *Yield: 2 dozen*

ALICE MARUM
KINGSTON, NOVA SCOTIA

MAPLE-WALNUT CHIPPERS

Chocolate chip cookies with a New England twist.

2¼ cups flour
1 teaspoon baking soda
½ teaspoon salt
1 cup butter or margarine, room temperature
½ cup granulated sugar

½ cup brown sugar, firmly packed
¼ cup maple syrup
1 egg
½ cup walnuts, coarsely chopped
12 ounces (2 cups) semisweet chocolate chips

Mix together flour, baking soda, and salt, and set aside.

Cream together butter, sugars, maple syrup, and egg. Add the dry ingredients, and mix until blended. Stir in the nuts and chocolate chips.

Drop by teaspoonfuls onto ungreased baking sheets. Bake at 375°F. for 8 to 10 minutes until golden brown. Cool for a few minutes on the sheet, then remove to a rack to cool.   *Yield: 6 dozen*

DANITA YANNIELLO
BURBANK, CALIFORNIA

BLACK AND WHITE COOKIES

To keep these soft, coconut-chocolate chip cookies moist, place a slice of bread with them in a tightly covered container.

1¾ cups flour
½ cup unsweetened cocoa
1 teaspoon baking soda
½ teaspoon salt
1 cup butter, room temperature
1 cup brown sugar, firmly packed

⅓ cup granulated fructose
1½ teaspoons vanilla extract
2 eggs
12 ounces (2 cups) milk chocolate chips
⅔ cup sweetened flaked coconut

Combine flour, cocoa, baking soda, and salt, and set aside.

In a large bowl, beat butter, sugar, fructose, and vanilla with electric mixer on medium speed until fluffy. Beat in eggs until well blended. On low speed, gradually mix in dry ingredients just until well blended. With a wooden spoon, stir in chips and coconut.

Drop dough by heaping tablespoonfuls onto ungreased baking sheets. Bake at 350°F. for 10 to 12 minutes. Cool on baking sheets for about 1 minute before removing to racks to complete cooling.   *Yield: 3½ dozen*

AMY GARRETT
PRESCOTT VALLEY, ARIZONA

COCONUT CHOCOLATE CHIP COOKIES

The mild flavor of coconut is the perfect complement for chocolate chips and pecans. For best results, do not skimp on the chocolate—this recipe loads every cookie with plenty of chocolate chips.

2½ cups flour
1 teaspoon baking soda
1 teaspoon salt
¾ cup plus 2 tablespoons butter
2 tablespoons canned coconut cream
½ cup granulated sugar

1 cup brown sugar, firmly packed
2 eggs
1 teaspoon vanilla extract
2½ cups semisweet chocolate chips
1½ cups chopped pecans
½ cup sweetened flaked coconut

Mix flour, baking soda, and salt, and set aside.

In a large bowl, cream butter and coconut cream. Add sugars and beat until well mixed. Beat in the eggs and vanilla until the mixture is creamy. Stir dry ingredients into creamed mixture just until the flour is completely blended in. Stir in chocolate chips, pecans, and coconut until combined.

Drop by rounded tablespoonfuls onto greased baking sheets. Bake at 375°F. for 8 to 9 minutes. *Yield: 5 dozen*

BRIDGET MCDONOUGH
CHICAGO, ILLINOIS

SOUR CREAM CHOCOLATE CHIP COOKIES I

2 cups flour
1 teaspoon baking soda
1 teaspoon salt
1 cup butter or margarine, softened
1 cup granulated sugar
½ cup brown sugar, firmly packed

2 eggs
2 teaspoons vanilla extract
⅓ cup sour cream
1 cup chopped nuts
12 ounces (2 cups) semisweet chocolate chips

Sift together the flour, baking soda, and salt, and set aside.

Combine butter, sugars, eggs, and vanilla, and beat until creamy. Add sifted ingredients, and blend well. Add nuts and chocolate chips.

Drop by teaspoonfuls onto ungreased baking sheets. Bake at 350°F. for 8 to 10 minutes. *Yield: about 4 dozen*

AGNES M. LAFLIN
TEMPE, ARIZONA

SOUR CREAM CHOCOLATE CHIP COOKIES II

Because these cookies have a cakelike texture, the sugar does not carmelize and the cookies do not brown like other chocolate chip cookies.

2 to 2½ cups flour
1 teaspoon baking powder
½ teaspoon baking soda
dash of salt
¾ cup plus 2 tablespoons sugar

½ cup butter or margarine, melted
1 egg
½ cup sour cream
1 teaspoon vanilla extract
12 ounces (2 cups) semisweet chocolate chips

Sift together 1 cup flour, baking powder, baking soda, and salt, and set aside.

Cream together sugar and butter. Add egg and mix well. Add sour cream; mix until smooth and no lumps of sour cream appear. Add vanilla. Stir sifted ingredients into butter and sugar mixture. Add the remaining flour gradually until a semifirm but smooth consistency is obtained.

Add chocolate chips and mix well.

Drop by teaspoonfuls onto greased baking sheets. Bake at 375°F. for 12 to 15 minutes until *lightly* golden. Remember, these cookies will not brown, so be careful not to overbake.
Yield: 4 to 6 dozen

TRICIA MALANKA
PACIFIC GROVE, CALIFORNIA

YOGURT-PECAN CHOCOLATE CHIP COOKIES

A cakey, pecan- and chocolate-filled delight, these cookies are best served very fresh. Yogurt accounts in part for their distinctive flavor and cakelike texture.

1¾ cups flour
¾ teaspoon baking soda
¼ teaspoon salt
½ cup unsalted (sweet) butter, room temperature
1 cup plus 2 tablespoons sugar
2 tablespoons molasses

1½ teaspoons vanilla extract
1 large egg
½ cup plain, whole-milk yogurt
¾ cup broken pecan pieces
1½ cups semisweet chocolate chips

Sift flour before measuring, then resift with baking soda and salt, and set aside.

In a large mixing bowl, cream butter until fluffy. Add sugar, beating until well blended. Add molasses, vanilla, and egg, and blend thoroughly. Add about one cup of sifted ingredients, and mix well. Blend in yogurt. Add remaining sifted ingredients, stirring to blend thoroughly. Stir in nuts and chocolate chips.

Drop by rounded tablespoonfuls onto baking sheets lined with lightly greased aluminum foil. Bake at 350°F. for about 12 minutes, until cookies are just turning golden brown. Remove from baking sheets to cool.   *Yield: about 2½ dozen*

LISA DE MAURO
YONKERS, NEW YORK

MOCHA DREAMS

Coffee and chocolate have a natural affinity for each other, and this recipe for eggless, coffee-flavored cookies capitalizes on the mutual attraction. Since these cookies do not spread, they are a good choice when you need a lot of small, bite-sized cookies.

2½ cups flour
½ teaspoon baking powder
¼ teaspoon salt
1 cup unsalted (sweet) butter
1 cup brown sugar

1 teaspoon vanilla extract
1 tablespoon instant coffee granules
12 ounces (2 cups) semisweet chocolate chips
1 cup chopped pecans or walnuts

Sift together flour, baking powder, and salt. Set aside.

In a large bowl cream together butter and brown sugar. Blend in vanilla and coffee granules. Add sifted ingredients to creamed mixture and mix well. Stir in chocolate and nuts.

Drop by teaspoonfuls onto lightly buttered baking sheets. Bake at 350°F. for 8 to 10 minutes, or until lightly browned. Cool slightly before removing from baking trays. *Yield: about 6 dozen*

BARBARA NOWAKOWSKI
NORTH TONAWANDA, NEW YORK

PUDDING & SWEET CHOCOLATE CHIPS

2¼ cups flour
1 teaspoon baking soda
1 cup butter, softened
¼ cup granulated sugar
¾ cup light brown sugar, firmly packed

1 teaspoon vanilla extract
1 package (4-serving size) instant vanilla pudding
2 eggs
2 4-ounce bars sweet baking chocolate, broken into small pieces

Mix flour with baking soda, and set aside.

Combine butter, sugars, vanilla, and pudding mix in large mixing bowl, and beat until smooth and creamy. Beat in eggs. Gradually add dry ingredients. Gently stir in broken chocolate pieces.

Drop by rounded teaspoonfuls onto ungreased baking sheets, placing cookies about 2 inches apart. Bake at 350°F. for 15 to 20 minutes. *Yield: 6 dozen*

JOAN LEHMAN
COLUMBUS, OHIO

MILK CHOCOLATE CHIP DELIGHTS

A melt-in-your-mouth cookie featuring milk chocolate morsels.

2¼ cup flour, unsifted
1 teaspoon baking soda
1 cup margarine, softened
¼ cup granulated sugar
¾ cup light brown sugar, firmly packed

1 teaspoon vanilla extract
1 package (4-serving size) instant vanilla pudding
   mix
2 eggs
12 ounces (2 cups) milk chocolate morsels

Sift together the flour and baking soda, and set aside.

Combine margarine, the sugars, vanilla, and pudding mix in food processor until smooth and creamy. Beat in the eggs. Gradually blend in sifted ingredients; batter will be stiff. Gently stir in chocolate morsels.

Drop by rounded teaspoonfuls onto ungreased baking sheets, placing cookies about 2 inches apart. Flatten a bit with the back of a fork; these cookies spread very little while baking. Bake at 375°F. for 8 to 10 minutes.   *Yield: 5 to 7 dozen*

BETTY LANDERS
MORGANTON, NORTH CAROLINA

TIGER-STRIPED CHOCOLATE CHIP COOKIES

2½ cups flour
1 teaspoon baking soda
¼ teaspoon salt
8 ounces tub margarine
½ cup creamy peanut butter
1 cup granulated sugar

1 cup brown sugar, firmly packed
2 eggs
1 teaspoon vanilla extract
8-ounce milk chocolate bar, cut into ¼- to ½-inch
    chunks
6 ounces (1 cup) semisweet chocolate chips

Sift together flour, baking soda, and salt, and set aside.

Cream margarine, peanut butter, and sugars until light and fluffy. Beat in eggs and vanilla. Add sifted ingredients, and mix well. Gently stir in milk chocolate chunks.

Melt chocolate chips over very low heat. Care-fully stir melted chocolate into cookie dough. Do *not* blend into dough; chocolate should be swirled in just enough to make stripes.

Drop by teaspoonfuls onto ungreased baking sheets. Bake at 350°F. for 10 to 12 minutes. Cool slightly before removing from baking sheets. Store in airtight container.   *Yield: 4 dozen*

SANNA TECHAU
CYNTHIANA, KENTUCKY

KEEP YOUR OPTIONS OPEN

A little of this, or a little more of that—vary this recipe to suit your mood! For best results, however, do not substitute margarine for the butter called for.

3 cups flour
1 teaspoon baking soda
1 teaspoon salt
⅓ cup shortening
1 cup butter, softened
1 cup granulated sugar
1 cup brown sugar, firmly packed
2 eggs
2 teaspoons vanilla extract

½ teaspoon coconut flavoring (optional)
½ teaspoon almond extract (optional)
1 cup chopped pecans or almonds (or a combination of both)
9 to 12 ounces (1½ to 2 cups) milk chocolate chips or semisweet chocolate chips
4 to 6 ounces (¾ to 1 cup) butterscotch chips (optional)

Mix together flour, baking soda, and salt, and set aside.

Beat shortening, butter, sugars, and eggs until well blended. Add flavorings. Gradually add dry ingredients, a cup at a time, mixing well after each addition. Fold in nuts and chips. Refrigerate for 2 hours or overnight.

Drop dough by teaspoonfuls onto greased baking sheets. Bake at 375°F. for 12 to 14 minutes. Cool on racks.

Final option: For a special treat, roll teaspoon-sized balls of dough in a mixture of cinnamon and sugar (2 tablespoons sugar to ½ tablespoon cinnamon) before baking as directed above.
Yield: 4 to 5 dozen

ROSE KEGLER HALLARN
COLUMBUS, OHIO

DOUBLE PEANUT BUTTER CHOCOLATE CHIP COOKIES

Triple-power nuttiness with peanut butter, peanut butter chips, and pecans all in one chocolate chip cookie.

2 cups flour
2 teaspoons baking soda
½ cup butter or margarine
1 cup granulated sugar
1 cup brown sugar, firmly packed
2 eggs

1 teaspoon vanilla extract
1 cup chunky peanut butter
½ cup chopped pecans
6 ounces (1 cup) semisweet chocolate chips
6 ounces (1 cup) peanut butter chips

Sift flour before measuring, then resift with baking soda, and set aside.

With an electric mixer, cream together butter and sugars. Beat in eggs and vanilla. Add peanut butter, and beat until well mixed.

Stir in sifted ingredients. Add pecans, chocolate chips, and peanut butter chips.

Drop by teaspoonfuls onto greased baking sheets. Bake at 350°F. for about 12 minutes. *Yield: 4½ dozen*

JOAN WHITSON WALLACE
SEVERN, MARYLAND

HAZELNUT BUTTER CHOCOLATE CHIP COOKIES

This cookie originated in Oregon's hazelnut country, where the availability of hazelnut butter offers a rich and unusual alternative to peanut butter. In some parts of the country hazelnuts are called filberts.

1½ cups flour
¾ teaspoon baking soda
½ teaspoon baking powder
¼ teaspoon salt
1 cup crunchy hazelnut butter or peanut butter
½ cup butter or margarine

½ cup granulated sugar
½ cup brown sugar, firmly packed
½ teaspoon vanilla extract
1 egg
12 ounces (2 cups) semisweet chocolate chips

Sift together the flour, baking soda, baking powder, and salt. Set aside.

Cream hazelnut butter, butter, and sugars together until very light and fluffy. Beat in vanilla and eggs. Stir in the sifted ingredients and mix well. Stir in chocolate chips.

Chill 2 hours. Drop by tablespoonfuls onto baking sheets. Bake at 375°F. for 10 to 12 minutes. ***Yield: 4½ to 5 dozen***

VERNA KASTNER
HILLSBORO, OREGON

... AND THEY'RE GOOD FOR YOU, TOO

Snacks, even spectacularly good-tasting ones, needn't be empty

calories. When something is as quickly devoured as a batch of

freshly baked chocolate chip cookies, why not lace it with

wholesome ingredients that will not only take the edge off after-

school appetites, but also provide a healthy dose of things that

are good for bodies as well: nuts and nut butters, rolled oats

and other whole grains, wheat germ and bran, dried fruits,

yogurt, honey, and even such improbable ingredients as

pinto beans and zucchini.

SUNNY CHOCOLATE CHIP COOKIES

1¼ cups all-purpose flour
1 cup whole wheat flour
1 teaspoon baking soda
½ teaspoon baking powder
¼ teaspoon salt
1 cup butter or margarine, softened
¾ cup granulated sugar

¾ cup brown sugar, firmly packed
2 eggs
1 teaspoon vanilla extract
12 ounces (2 cups) semisweet chocolate chips
½ cup salted sunflower kernels
¼ cup sesame seeds

Combine flours, baking soda, baking powder, and salt; set aside.

Cream butter. Gradually add sugars, beating until light and fluffy. Add eggs and vanilla, and beat well. Add dry ingredients to creamed mixture, and beat well. Stir in remaining ingredients in the order given.

Drop dough by heaping teaspoonfuls onto lightly greased baking sheets. Bake at 375°F. for 8 to 10 minutes. Cool slightly on baking sheets before removing to wire racks. *Yield: 5 dozen*

MARILYN TAYLOR
WINFIELD, KANSAS

WHOLE GRAIN & HONEY CHOCOLATE CHIP COOKIES

2¼ cups whole wheat flour
1 teaspoon baking soda
1 teaspoon salt
1 cup butter, margarine, or shortening, softened
⅔ cup honey

¼ cup powdered milk
1 teaspoon vanilla extract
2 eggs
12 ounces (2 cups) semisweet chocolate morsels
½ to 1 cup walnuts, finely chopped

Sift together the flour, baking soda, and salt, and set aside.

Beat the butter, honey, powdered milk, and vanilla until creamy. Add eggs. Add sifted ingredients and blend well. Stir in chocolate chips and walnuts.

Drop by small teaspoonfuls onto lightly greased baking sheets. Bake at 375°F. for 10 to 12 minutes. Bake only until lightly browned or bottoms will burn.   *Yield: about 3 dozen*

DIANA K. STAVA
NEWBERG, OREGON

OH-YUM CHOCOLATE CHIP FACTORY COOKIES

The fourteen-year-old creator of this recipe makes up batches of 19 dozen cookies at a time for sale to local schools and businesses. She calls her business the "Oh-yum Chocolate-Chip Factory" and has recently been joined in the enterprise by her ten-year-old brother.

1⅔ cups all-purpose flour
1½ cups whole wheat flour
1 teaspoon baking soda
1 teaspoon salt
1 cup margarine or shortening
1 cup granulated sugar

1 cup brown sugar
2 eggs
2 tablespoons hot water
2½ teaspoons vanilla extract
12 ounces (2 cups) semisweet chocolate chips
1 cup chopped nuts

Sift together flours, baking soda, and salt; set aside.

Cream margarine and sugars. Add eggs, hot water and vanilla. Beat until fluffy. Stir in sifted ingredients. Gently add chocolate chips and nuts.

Drop by teaspoonfuls onto greased baking sheets. Bake at 375°F. for 8 to 10 minutes or until light brown.   *Yield: 5 to 6 dozen*

CAROL JOY BRENDLINGER
PORTLAND, OREGON

CHOCOLATE CHIP COOKIES WITH BRAN

The addition of bran to the traditional chocolate chip cookie formula makes a pleasant textural change and adds healthful fiber to this dessert or snack.

1¼ cups flour
1 teaspoon baking soda
1 teaspoon salt
1 cup unsalted (sweet) butter, room temperature
¾ cup granulated sugar
¾ cup light brown sugar, firmly packed

1 teaspoon vanilla extract
2 eggs
12 ounces (2 cups) semisweet chocolate chips
½ cup finely chopped pecans
½ cup bran

Sift the flour before measuring, then resift with baking soda and salt; set aside.

Cream butter, sugars, and vanilla together until smooth. Add eggs. Stir in sifted ingredients, and mix until well blended. Gently stir in chocolate chips, pecans, and bran.

Form dough into balls the size of large walnuts. Place on lightly greased baking sheets, allowing room between cookies for expansion. Press down on balls with lightly water-moistened fingers to flatten. Bake at 350°F. for 10 to 12 minutes.   *Yield: 4 dozen*

MARILYN TAYLOR
WINFIELD, KANSAS

NUTRILICIOUS TRIPLE CHOCOLATE CHIP COOKIES

Having grown up on a large wheat farm in Saskatchewan, Canada, the creator of this recipe appreciates the magic that wholesome, fresh ingredients put into any recipe.

1 cup old-fashioned rolled oats
1¾ cups flour
1 teaspoon baking soda
⅛ teaspoon salt
½ cup wheat germ
½ cup coconut

1 cup butter, softened
1½ cups brown sugar, firmly packed
1½ teaspoons vanilla extract
2 large eggs
12 ounces (2 cups) semisweet chocolate chips
1 cup chopped walnuts

Place rolled oats in blender and whirl at low speed for about 15 seconds. Combine rolled oats, flour, baking soda, salt, wheat germ, and coconut, and set aside.

Cream together butter, sugar, and vanilla until smooth. Beat in eggs. Gradually add dry ingredients to creamed mixture, and combine well. Stir in chocolate chips and nuts.

Drop batter by well-rounded teaspoonfuls onto ungreased baking sheets. Bake at 375°F. for 10 to 12 minutes.   *Yield: 6½ dozen*

ADELE A. CHATFIELD
PORTLAND, OREGON

WHOLE-GRAIN CHOCOLATE CHIP COOKIES

This hearty cookie recipe originated in Germany many years ago. For best results, use a real Irish oatmeal, such as McCann's Quick-Cooking Irish Oatmeal.

1 cup unbleached, all-purpose flour
1 cup stone-ground whole wheat flour
1 teaspoon baking soda
½ teaspoon baking powder
pinch of salt
1 cup granulated sugar
1 cup light brown sugar

1 cup butter (or ½ butter and ½ margarine, or 1 cup shortening)
2 eggs
1 teaspoon vanilla extract
2 cups quick-cooking, rolled oats
12 ounces (2 cups) semisweet chocolate chips

Sift together flours, baking soda, baking powder, and salt; set aside.

Cream together sugars and butter. Add eggs. Add sifted ingredients to creamed mixture. Stir in vanilla, oatmeal, and chocolate chips.

Drop by teaspoonfuls onto lightly greased baking sheets. Bake at 375°F. for 8 to 10 minutes. Allow cookies to cool slightly on trays before removing to racks to cool completely.   *Yield: about 4 dozen*

SHEILA NUSBAUM
RICHMOND, VIRGINIA

OATMEAL CHOCOLATE CHIP COOKIES I

*Melting the butter before adding it to the other ingredients causes the cookies
to spread more while baking.*

½ cup rolled oats
2 cups flour
1 teaspoon baking soda
1 cup butter, melted and cooled slightly
¾ cup granulated sugar

¾ cup brown sugar, firmly packed
2 eggs
1 teaspoon vanilla extract
1 cup semisweet chocolate chips
1 cup chopped walnuts

Place rolled oats in blender and grind until fine. Measure out ¼ cup and sift it together with flour and baking soda. Set aside.

Mix together the melted butter, sugars, and eggs; blend until smooth. Stir in vanilla. Stir in sifted ingredients and mix well. Add chocolate chips and walnuts.

Drop by rounded tablespoonfuls onto greased baking sheets. Bake at 350°F. in convection oven for 10 to 12 minutes, or at 375°F. in regular oven for about 10 minutes.   *Yield: about 3 dozen*

CAROLE EVANS
BURIEN, WASHINGTON

OATMEAL CHOCOLATE CHIP COOKIES II

Shortening and extra egg yolks make a soft, chewy cookie.

2¼ cups flour
1 teaspoon baking soda
1 teaspoon salt
½ cup butter, softened
½ cup shortening
¾ cup granulated sugar
¾ cup brown sugar, firmly packed

1 teaspoon vanilla extract
1 whole egg
2 egg yolks
¼ cup rolled oats
12 ounces (2 cups) semisweet chocolate chips
1 cup nuts, chopped

Combine flour, baking soda, and salt; set aside.

In a large bowl, combine butter, shortening, sugars, and vanilla, and cream until fluffy. Add egg and egg yolks; beat well.

Gradually add all but about ½ cup dry ingredients. Mix rolled oats with remaining flour, and stir into batter. Stir in chocolate chips and nuts.

Drop by heaping teaspoonfuls onto ungreased baking sheets. Bake at 375°F. for 10 to 12 minutes.   *Yield: about 5 dozen*

CAROL CAMPBELL
MIDWEST CITY, OKLAHOMA

OATMEAL CHOCOLATE CHIP COOKIES III

This old family recipe, which has been updated over the years first with raisins, then with chocolate chips, comes from a tradition where the cookie jar is the symbol of family hospitality and cookies the reward for almost everything.

1 cup quick-cooking rolled oats
⅓ cup flour
1 teaspoon baking powder
¼ teaspoon salt
½ cup sugar
1 egg, well-beaten

1 tablespoon corn oil
1 teaspoon vanilla extract
½ cup shredded coconut
6 ounces (1 cup) semisweet chocolate chips
½ cup chopped nuts

Stir together the rolled oats, flour, baking powder, salt, and sugar. Mix in the beaten egg. Add the corn oil and vanilla, and blend well. Stir in coconut, chocolate chips, and nuts, and mix well.

Drop by teaspoonfuls onto lightly oiled baking sheets, spacing cookies about 2 inches apart. Bake at 350°F. for 8 to 10 minutes. Remove from pans to cooling racks while still hot.
Yield: about 3 dozen

IRENE G. CARTER
EL PASO, TEXAS

ONCE-AROUND-THE-KITCHEN COOKIES

2 cups flour
1 teaspoon baking soda
1 cup butter
½ cup peanut butter
½ cup granulated sugar
1 cup brown sugar, firmly packed

2 eggs
1½ cups rolled oats
½ cup chopped walnuts
½ cup raisins
12 ounces (2 cups) semisweet chocolate chips
½ cup flaked coconut

Combine flour and baking soda, and set aside.
Cream butter, peanut butter, and sugars. Beat in eggs. Add rolled oats, walnuts, raisins, chocolate chips, and coconut. Add dry ingredients and mix thoroughly.

Drop by teaspoonfuls onto ungreased baking sheets. Bake at 375°F. for about 10 minutes. *Yield: 2½ dozen*

SANDY PAULSRUD
NIELSVILLE, MINNESOTA

COWGIRL COOKIES

4 cups flour
2 teaspoons baking soda
1 teaspoon baking powder
1 teaspoon salt
2 cups shortening
2 cups granulated sugar

2 cups brown sugar, firmly packed
4 eggs
3 cups quick-cooking, rolled oats
2 teaspoons vanilla extract
12 ounces (2 cups) semisweet chocolate chips

Sift together the flour, baking soda, baking powder, and salt, and set aside.

Combine the shortening and sugars, and cream well. Beat in eggs until thoroughly blended. Stir in dry ingredients and mix well. Add oats, vanilla, and chocolate chips.

Drop by teaspoonfuls onto greased baking sheets. Bake at 350°F. for about 12 minutes or until golden brown.   *Yield: 8 dozen*

BEV ALMAGUER AND NANCY FRY
FARGO, NORTH DAKOTA

OATMEAL MILK CHOCOLATE CHUNK COOKIES

Although these cookies may not appear done at the end of baking time, do not overbake. They are meant to be soft cookies, and overbaking will ruin them.

2 cups flour
1 teaspoon baking powder
1 teaspoon baking soda
2½ cups rolled oats
1 cup unsalted (sweet) butter, softened
1 cup granulated sugar

1 cup brown sugar, firmly packed
2 eggs
1 teaspoon vanilla extract
12 ounces (2 cups) semisweet chocolate chips
8-ounce milk chocolate bar, grated
1½ cups chopped nuts

Sift together the flour, baking powder, and baking soda, and set aside.

Whirl rolled oats in food processor or blender until reduced to fine powder. Mix into other dry ingredients, and set aside.

Cream butter and sugars. Blend in eggs until smooth and creamy. Stir in vanilla. Gradually add sifted ingredients to creamed mixture, stirring well after each addition; batter will be stiff. Mix in the chocolate chips, grated chocolate, and nuts.

Place golf ball-sized pieces of dough about 2 inches apart on an ungreased baking sheet. Do not flatten dough. Bake at 400°F. for about 8 minutes. *Do not overbake.*   *Yield: 2 dozen*

EDRY NADDOUR GOOT
PHOENIX, ARIZONA

GRAMMA'S CHOCO-O-CHIPS

½ cup margarine
½ cup shortening
1 cup granulated sugar
½ cup brown sugar
1 teaspoon salt
1 teaspoon baking soda
2 eggs

1 teaspoon vanilla extract
2 cups quick-cooking rolled oats
1⅓ cups all-purpose flour (or more to make stiff dough)
1 cup semisweet chocolate chips
1 cup chocolate chunks or large chips

Mix thoroughly margarine, shortening, sugars, salt, baking soda, eggs, and vanilla. Add oats and flour. You will have a very stiff dough. Add chocolate chips and chunks.

Drop by teaspoonfuls onto ungreased baking sheets. Bake at 375°F. for 8 to 10 minutes. *Yield: about 4 dozen*

CATHERINE RIVERS
DALTON, MASSACHUSETTS

CHOCO-O'S

Try adding raisins or, at Christmas, some chopped candied fruit to this cookie dough.

2 cups flour
1 teaspoon baking soda
2 cups quick-cooking, rolled oats
1 cup butter or margarine
1 cup granulated sugar
1 cup brown sugar, packed

2 eggs
1 teaspoon vanilla extract
½ teaspoon almond extract
1 cup chopped nuts
2 cups semisweet chocolate chips

Sift flour and baking soda together; add oats. Set aside.

Cream butter and sugars. Add eggs one at a time, beating after each addition until creamy. Fold in sifted ingredients. Stir in vanilla and almond extracts. Gently mix in nuts and chocolate chips.

Drop by teaspoonfuls onto greased baking sheets, placing cookies 2 inches apart. Bake at 375°F. for 10 to 12 minutes, or until lightly browned.   *Yield: 5 dozen*

JESSE B. PYLE
MARINE CITY, MISSISSIPPI

OATMEAL AND SOUR CREAM CHOCOLATE CHIP COOKIES

A rich cookie with rolled oats and sour cream for texture and flavor.

2 cups flour
1 teaspoon baking soda
½ teaspoon salt
1 cup rolled oats
1¼ cups light brown sugar, firmly packed
1 cup unsalted (sweet) butter or margarine
2 eggs

1 teaspoon vanilla extract
½ cup sour cream
12 ounces (2 cups) semisweet chocolate chips
12 ounces (2 cups) milk chocolate morsels
¼ cup raisins
¾ cup walnuts, coarsely chopped
¾ cup pecans, coarsely chopped

Sift flour, baking soda, and salt together; stir in rolled oats. Set aside.

In a large bowl, cream together sugar and butter until light and fluffy. Beat in eggs and vanilla. Add sifted ingredients to creamed mixture until just blended. Add sour cream and mix until just blended. Stir in chocolates, raisins, and nuts.

Drop dough by heaping teaspoonfuls onto ungreased baking sheets, placing cookies 2 inches apart. Bake at 350°F. for 12-15 minutes, or until lightly browned around the edges. Allow to cool on cookie sheets for 5 minutes before removing to racks to cool completely.   *Yield: about 5½ dozen*

MARIANNE MCBRIDE
PACIFICA, CALIFORNIA

PEANUT BUTTER & OATMEAL CHOCOLATE CHIP COOKIES

Use a light touch while working with this dough: do not overbeat and do not overbake.

3 cups flour
3 teaspoons baking soda
1½ teaspoons salt
1½ cups quick-cooking, rolled oats
1½ cups granulated sugar
1½ cups brown sugar

1½ cups margarine
1½ cups peanut butter
1½ teaspoons vanilla extract
3 eggs
12 ounces (2 cups) semisweet chocolate chips
1 cup chopped nuts

Sift flour, baking soda, and salt together. Stir in rolled oats, and set aside.

Cream together sugars, margarine, and peanut butter. Add vanilla and eggs, and beat well. Add sifted ingredients and mix well. Add chocolate chips and nuts. Chill for 2 hours.

Form dough into walnut-sized balls and place on ungreased baking sheets. Bake at 375°F. for 10 to 12 minutes. Do not overbake.   *Yield: 5 to 6 dozen*

LOVELL MCGILLICUDDY
CEDAR RAPIDS, IOWA

MOLASSES-OATMEAL CHOCOLATE CHIP COOKIES

A favorite family recipe features the old-fashioned taste of molasses and spices.

1½ cups flour
1 teaspoon baking soda
½ teaspoon ground cloves
½ teaspoon ginger
½ teaspoon salt
1 cup sugar

¾ cup butter
1 egg
¼ cup dark molasses
¾ cup quick-cooking rolled oats
½ cup raisins
6 ounces (1 cup) semisweet chocolate chips

Sift flour before measuring, then resift with baking soda, cloves, ginger, salt, and sugar; set aside.

Cream butter and egg. Add sifted ingredients and beat with electric mixer until smooth, about 2 minutes.

Blend in molasses, rolled oats, raisins, and chocolate chips. Dough will be quite sticky.

Drop by rounded tablespoonfuls onto ungreased baking sheets. Bake at 375°F. for 8 to 10 minutes. Cool before removing from baking sheets. *Yield: 2 dozen*

MRS. HARRIET A. KEMP
SEATTLE, WASHINGTON

GRANOLA CHOCOLATE CHIP COOKIES

A rather hard, crisp, granola-like cookie that stores well in airtight canisters or zip-lock bags.

2 cups flour
2 teaspoons baking soda
1 teaspoon baking powder
½ teaspoon salt
1 cup shortening
1 cup granulated sugar
1 cup light brown sugar, firmly packed

1 teaspoon vanilla extract
2 eggs
2 cups rolled oats
2 cups corn flakes
1 cup shredded coconut
1 cup salted peanuts
6 ounces (1 cup) semisweet chocolate chips

Sift together the flour, baking soda, baking powder, and salt; set aside.

Beat together the shortening, sugars, and vanilla until light and creamy. Add eggs one at a time, mixing thoroughly after each addition. Blend until uniform in color.

Add the sifted ingredients, one-half cup at a time, mixing thoroughly after each addition. Add remaining ingredients, one by one, in the order they are listed. Mix with your hands, as the mixture will be stiff and dry. Push the mixture together in a tight ball to insure thorough mixing.

Pinch off 2-inch balls, and roll them tightly. Place cookies on ungreased baking sheets, and press into button shapes. Bake at 350°F. for 12 to 15 minutes, cooking only as many sheets at one time as will allow good air circulation in the oven. Cookies will be golden brown. Cool cookies on sheets for 2 or 3 minutes; remove to wire racks to finish cooling.   *Yield: about 5 dozen*

D. MICHAEL PITALO
BATON ROUGE, LOUISIANA

PACIFIC PRIDE CHOCOLATE CHIP COOKIES

Created by an anthropologist who enjoys seeing the connection between food and where it is grown, this recipe takes its name from the West Coast and Pacific island sources of many of its ingredients: Hawaiian sugars, Washington State wheats, South Pacific coconuts, and Oregon hazelnuts. Milk chocolate was chosen rather than semisweet chocolate to better complement those famous Oregon hazelnuts. Hazelnuts should be spread on a baking sheet and toasted lightly in a 350°F. oven before adding to dough.

2 cups flour
1 cup margarine
1 cup granulated sugar
1 cup brown sugar
2 eggs
1 teaspoon vanilla extract
1 teaspoon baking soda

½ teaspoon baking powder
¼ teaspoon salt
2 cups rolled oats
1 cup bran, corn, or wheat flakes
1 cup coconut
1 cup hazelnuts, chopped
1 generous cup milk chocolate chips

Sift flour and set aside.

In a very large bowl, cream margarine, sugars, and eggs. Add vanilla, baking soda, baking powder, and salt. Add flour and mix well.

Stir in all remaining ingredients and mix well.

Drop by teaspoonfuls onto greased baking sheets. Bake at 300°F. for 12 minutes. *Yield: 6½ dozen*

SHIRLEY EWART
TIGARD, OREGON

NUTRITIOUS CHOCOLATE CHIP COOKIES

Try different combinations of the suggested optional ingredients for a great tasting cookie every time.

2¼ cups flour
2 cups brown sugar, firmly packed
1 teaspoon baking soda
1 cup butter or margarine, softened
2 teaspoons vanilla extract
2 eggs
2 cups rolled oats
12 ounces (2 cups) semisweet chocolate chips
½ cup nuts or sunflower seeds

Optional ingredients (use one or more of the following):
1 cup peanut butter
1 cup wheat germ
1 cup flaked coconut
1 cup dry milk

Combine 1¼ cups flour, brown sugar, baking soda, butter, vanilla, and eggs, and beat with electric mixer at medium speed until well blended. Stir in remaining ingredients by hand.

Drop dough by rounded teaspoonfuls onto ungreased cookie sheets, placing cookies about 2 inches apart. Bake at 350°F. for 10 minutes or until done.   *Yield: 6 to 7 dozen*

DONNA SMYRK
ROCHESTER, MINNESOTA

MOCHA PINTO CHIPPERS

Vary this recipe by substituting chopped dates or chopped golden raisins for the apricots.

1-pound can pinto beans, well drained
2 cups flour
1 teaspoon baking soda
½ teaspoon salt
1½ teaspoons instant coffee granules
3 tablespoons unsweetened cocoa
1 cup quick-cooking rolled oats
½ cup plus 2 teaspoons unsalted (sweet) butter, divided

½ cup shortening
¾ cup granulated sugar
1 cup brown sugar, firmly packed
¼ cup honey
1 egg
1 teaspoon vanilla extract
15 ounces (2½ cups) semisweet chocolate chips, divided
½ cup chopped dried apricots

Puree drained pinto beans in blender, food processor, or food ricer. Measure 1 cup and set aside.

In a large bowl, combine flour, baking soda, salt, coffee granules, cocoa, and oats. Set aside.

Cream together ½ cup butter and shortening. Gradually add sugars and honey, beating until fluffy. Add egg, vanilla, and bean puree. Mix to blend thoroughly. Stir in dry ingredients, and mix until completely blended. Gently stir in 1½ cups chocolate chips and chopped apricots.

Drop by tablespoonfuls onto lightly greased baking sheets. Flatten slightly with back of spoon. Bake at 350°F. for 15 to 18 minutes. Bake slightly longer for firmer, crisper cookie. Remove to wire racks to cool.

Melt together remaining chocolate chips and butter. Drizzle across cookies in a zig-zag pattern. Allow chocolate to set before storing cookies. *Yield: 5 dozen*

MARGARET RHODES
PRESCOTT, ARIZONA

ZESTY ZUCCHINI CHOCOLATE CHIP COOKIES

Have you ever dreamed of adding zucchini to your chocolate chip cookies? This recipe origi-nated in just that way. Rich in spices and chocolate, it is sure to be a conversation starter.

1¼ cups all-purpose flour
1¼ cups whole wheat flour
2 teaspoons baking powder
¼ teaspoon baking soda
¼ teaspoon salt
1 teaspoon cinnamon
½ teaspoon nutmeg
½ teaspoon ginger
½ teaspoon ground cloves

¼ cup unsalted (sweet) butter, softened
½ cup granulated sugar
1 cup light brown sugar, firmly packed
1 egg
1 teaspoon orange extract
1½ cups grated zucchini
1 cup chopped walnuts
6 ounces (1 cup) semisweet chocolate chips

Sift together flours, baking powder, baking soda, salt, cinnamon, nutmeg, ginger, and cloves. Set aside.

In a large mixing bowl, beat butter and sugars until light and fluffy. Beat in egg and orange extract. Add grated zucchini and mix well. Add dry sifted ingredients stirring until well blended. Gently fold in walnuts and chocolate chips.

Drop by tablespoonfuls onto greased baking sheets, spacing cookies well apart. Bake at 350°F. for about 12 minutes or until lightly brown. *Yield: 6½ dozen*

CHRISTINE E. SHAMANOFF
FORT WAYNE, INDIANA

DOUBLE CHOCOLATE
CHIP COOKIES

We now enter the realm of the serious chocolate eaters—those
who believe that if some chocolate is good, twice as much is
better; those who find chocolate chips alone inadequate to
satisfy their longings, and desire their chocolate chips
surrounded by rich, chocolate cookie as well.

DOUBLE CHOCOLATE CHIP COOKIES I

The grand prize-winning recipe of all 2600 submitted to The Orchards' contest in 1987 is this rich, moist, double chocolate cookie. The cookies were judged by three editors from Chocolatier, Orchards pastry chef Heather Andrus, and owners of the inn, Chester and Carol Soling. Each judge had three minutes to savor each cookie and rank it on a scale of one to ten. Sips of cold milk, water, or champagne cleared their palates for the next tasting.

1¾ cups flour
¼ teaspoon baking soda
1 cup butter or margarine, softened
1 teaspoon vanilla extract
1 cup granulated sugar
½ cup dark brown sugar, firmly packed

1 egg
⅓ cup unsweetened cocoa
2 tablespoons milk
1 cup chopped pecans or walnuts
6 ounces (1 cup) semisweet chocolate chips

Combine flour and baking soda, and set aside. Use an electric mixer to cream butter. Add vanilla and sugars, and beat until fluffy. Beat in egg. At low speed beat in cocoa, then milk. With a wooden spoon mix in dry ingredients just until blended. Stir in nuts and chocolate chips.

Drop by rounded teaspoonfuls onto nonstick or foil-lined baking sheets. Bake at 350°F. for 12 to 13 minutes. Remove from oven and cool slightly before removing from baking sheets. *Yield: 3 dozen*

JUNIOR LEAGUE OF LAS VEGAS
LAS VEGAS, NEVADA

This recipe was first published in Winning at the Table *by the Junior League of Las Vegas.*

THE PERFECT CHOCOLATE CHIP COOKIE

DOUBLE CHOCOLATE CHIP COOKIES II

Soft and chewy, and likely to stay that way—if you can keep them.

3 cups flour
1 cup plus 2 tablespoons unsweetened cocoa
1½ teaspoons baking soda
¾ teaspoon salt
1¾ cups plus 2 tablespoons butter or margarine

3 cups sugar
3 eggs
1 teaspoon vanilla extract
12 ounces (2 cups) semisweet chocolate chips
1½ cups chopped pecans (optional)

Combine flour, cocoa, baking soda, and salt, and set aside.

Cream butter and sugar until light and fluffy. Add eggs and vanilla, and beat well. Blend dry ingredients into creamed mixture. Stir in chocolate chips and nuts.

Drop onto ungreased baking sheets. Bake at 350°F. for 8 or 9 minutes. Cookies will be soft. Cool slightly on baking sheet before removing to racks to cool completely before storing.   *Yield: 8 dozen*

CATHERINE C. THOMAS
COLUMBUS, OHIO

DOUBLE CHOCOLATE CHIP COOKIES III

Conceived by combining a brownie recipe with a chocolate chip cookie recipe, this is a creation for the chocolate fanatics among us—deep, rich chocolate through and through. Watch carefully while baking; these burn easily.

2¼ cups flour
¾ cup unsweetened cocoa
1 teaspoon baking soda
½ teaspoon salt
1¼ cups margarine
1½ cups sugar

2 tablespoons corn syrup
2 eggs
2 teaspoons vanilla extract
1 cup chopped nuts
2 cups semisweet chocolate chips

Combine flour, cocoa, baking soda, and salt, and set aside.

Cream margarine and sugar. Add corn syrup, eggs, and vanilla, and blend well. Gradually blend dry ingredients into creamed mixture. Stir in nuts and chocolate chips.

Drop by teaspoonfuls onto ungreased baking sheets. Bake at 350°F. for about 10 minutes. Do not overbake. Cookies will be soft and puffy while baking, but will flatten when cool.   *Yield: 4½ dozen*

MARJORIE GROSS
GREEN BAY, WISCONSIN

DOUBLE CHOCOLATE CHIP COOKIES IV

A soft, flavorful cookie.

2 cups flour
¼ cup unsweetened cocoa
½ teaspoon salt
1 cup margarine, room temperature
¾ cup granulated sugar
¾ cup brown sugar, firmly packed

2 eggs
1 teaspoon vanilla extract
1 teaspoon baking soda
1 tablespoon hot water
2 cups semisweet chocolate chips
2 cups chopped walnuts

Mix flour, cocoa, and salt, and set aside.

Cream margarine until smooth and add sugars. Add eggs and vanilla, and beat until pale and fluffy. Stir in *one-half* the dry ingredients.

In another bowl stir baking soda into water. Add this to the batter, then stir in remaining flour until well blended. Gently stir in chocolate chips and nuts.

Drop by heaping teaspoonfuls onto greased baking sheet (or cover baking sheet with ungreased piece of foil), placing cookies about 2 inches apart. Bake 10 to 12 minutes, or until cookies appear firm. *Yield: 3½ to 4 dozen cookies*

DOROTHY LENT
COLUMBUS, OHIO

DOUBLE CHOCOLATE CHIP COOKIES V

1¾ cups flour
¼ cup cocoa
1 teaspoon baking soda
½ teaspoon salt
½ cup granulated sugar
¾ cup brown sugar, firmly packed

1 cup butter, softened
1 teaspoon vanilla extract
1 egg
6 ounces (1 cup) semisweet chocolate chips
½ cup chopped nuts (optional)

Sift together flour, cocoa, baking soda, and salt, and set aside.

Cream together sugars and butter until light and fluffy. Blend in vanilla and egg. Add sifted ingredients to creamed mixture. Gently stir in chocolate chips and nuts.

Drop by teaspoonfuls onto ungreased baking sheets. Bake at 375°F. for 7 to 11 minutes, or until set. Do not overbake. Let cool 1 minute before removing from baking sheets. *Yield: 4 dozen*

GLORIA MacDONALD
CHADDS FORD, PENNSYLVANIA

BROWNIE CHOCOLATE CHIPS

A serendipitous combination of those two all-time favorites: brownies and chocolate chip cookies. This recipe is also delicious made with macadamia nuts or walnuts instead of pecans, and mint-chocolate chips, peanut butter chips, or butterscotch chips instead of semisweet chocolate chips. Or try substituting 1 teaspoon mint flavoring for 1 of the teaspoons of vanilla.

1⅓ cups flour
1 teaspoon baking powder
½ teaspoon salt
1 cup butter
4 1-ounce squares unsweetened chocolate

4 eggs
2 cups sugar
2 teaspoons vanilla extract
6 ounces (1 cup) semisweet chocolate chips
½ cup chopped pecans

Sift together flour, baking powder, and salt; set aside.

Melt butter and chocolate in double boiler; cool slightly.

With electric mixer beat eggs until well blended. Gradually add sugar and vanilla. Stir in choco-late mixture by hand. Stir in dry ingredients. Gently add chocolate chips.

Pour into greased 9 x 13 x 2-inch pan. Sprinkle nuts over top. Bake at 350°F. for 30 minutes. Cut while still warm. Store in the refrigerator.
Yield: about 24 bars

VICTORIA BAXTER
BIRMINGHAM, ALABAMA

FUDGE FANTASIES

1½ cups flour
½ teaspoon baking soda
¼ teaspoon salt
¼ cup unsweetened cocoa
½ cup butter

1¼ cups brown sugar, firmly packed
2 eggs
1 teaspoon vanilla extract
½ cup mini-semisweet chocolate chips
⅓ cup pecans, chopped

Sift together the flour, baking soda, salt, and cocoa. Set aside.

Cream the butter and sugar together until light. Add eggs one at a time, beating well after each addition. Add vanilla. Fold sifted ingredients into creamed mixture. Stir in nuts and chocolate chips.

Chill dough for one hour. Drop dough by teaspoonfuls onto greased baking sheets. Bake at 350°F. for 10 minutes. Cool slightly, but remove from baking sheets while still warm. *Yield: about 3 dozen*

CELIA A. KEEL
HUTCHINSON, KANSAS

BROWN AND WHITE CHOCOLATE CHIP COOKIES

1 cup flour
½ teaspoon baking powder
½ teaspoon salt
3 tablespoons unsweetened cocoa
½ cup shortening
¾ cup sugar

1 egg
½ teaspoon vanilla extract
6 ounces (1 cup) white chocolate, broken into small bits
½ cup chopped nuts

Mix together the flour, baking powder, salt, and cocoa; set aside.

Cream together the shortening and sugar. Add egg and vanilla, and beat until fluffy. Gradually add dry ingredients, mixing well. Add chocolate bits and nuts.

Drop by teaspoonfuls onto ungreased baking sheets. Bake at 375°F. for 10 minutes. *Yield: 2½ to 3 dozen*

FRANCES C. FULWIDER
CARMEL, NEW YORK

ICE CREAM CHOCOLATE CHIP COOKIES

Chocolate ice cream and unsweetened cocoa give this cookie a moist, fudgelike taste. To assure a moist cookie, be careful not to overbake. These cookies do not freeze well.

1¼ cups flour
½ teaspoon baking soda
½ teaspoon salt
¾ cup margarine, softened
½ cup granulated sugar
½ cup light brown sugar, firmly packed

⅓ cup unsweetened cocoa
1½ teaspoons vanilla extract
1 large egg
⅓ cup chocolate ice cream, softened
6 ounces (1 cup) semisweet chocolate chips
¾ cup coarsely chopped walnuts

Combine flour, baking soda, and salt; set aside.

In large mixing bowl, combine margarine, sugars, cocoa, and vanilla, and beat until creamy. Add egg and ice cream; beat well. Gradually add dry ingredients, and mix well. Stir in chocolate chips and walnuts.

Drop by well-rounded teaspoonfuls onto lightly greased baking sheets, placing cookies about 2 inches apart. Bake at 350°F. for 14 to 16 minutes until well set. Do not overbake.   *Yield: about 4 dozen*

GLORIA DUTRUMBLE
UNCASVILLE, CONNECTICUT

CHEESY DOUBLE CHOCOLATE CHIP COOKIES

Inspired by chocolate cheesecake and created to indulge a love for combined cream cheese and chocolate, these cookies taste even better the second day when the cheese has mellowed and the flavors have blended nicely. For variety try using mint or white chocolate chips in place of some or all of the semisweet chocolate chips.

3½ cups flour
½ cup unsweetened cocoa
1½ teaspoons baking soda
½ teaspoon salt
1 cup shortening
1 8-ounce package cream cheese, softened to room temperature

1 cup granulated sugar
1 cup brown sugar, firmly packed
3 extra large eggs
2 teaspoons vanilla extract
12 ounces (2 cups) semisweet chocolate chips
1 cup pecan pieces

Sift flour before measuring, then resift with cocoa, baking soda, and salt, and set aside.

Cream together shortening, cream cheese, and sugars. Add eggs one at a time, beating well after each addition. Add vanilla and mix well. Add sifted ingredients, and blend well. Stir in chocolate chips and nuts.

Drop by teaspoonfuls onto baking sheets lined with parchment paper. Bake at 350°F. for 10 to 12 minutes. Do not overbake.   *Yield: 3 to 4 dozen*

LYNDA L. HENDERSON
OGDEN, UTAH

DOUBLE CHOCOLATE

MAINLINERS

These are the cookies to bake when you need the most chocolate in a chocolate chip cookie . . . NOW! Though the combination of bittersweet and semisweet chocolate chips is inspired, in a real emergency all semisweet chips will suffice.

2 ounces unsweetened chocolate
¼ cup butter
¼ cup shortening
⅓ cup granulated sugar
½ cup dark brown sugar, firmly packed
1½ teaspoons vanilla extract
¼ teaspoon salt
2 eggs

½ teaspoon baking soda
½ teaspoon cream of tartar
¼ cup, plus 2 tablespoons rolled oats
¾ cup flour
⅔ cup walnuts, coarsely chopped
¾ cup bittersweet chocolate chunks
¾ cup semisweet chocolate chips

Carefully melt unsweetened chocolate in a small pan over very low heat. Set aside to cool.

In a large mixing bowl, combine butter, shortening, the sugars, vanilla, and salt. Beat until fluffy. Beat in eggs, baking soda, and cream of tartar. Stir in cooled chocolate.

Place rolled oats in blender or food processor, and grind into a fine powder. Add to batter along with flour. Stir in chopped nuts and chocolate chunks and chips.

Cover bowl and refrigerate for at least 4 hours.

Using about 2 tablespoons of dough per cookie, shape dough into balls. Place cookies on lightly greased baking sheets about 1½ inches apart. Bake at 325°F. for 10 to 12 minutes. Do not overbake. Cool on the sheets for 2 minutes. Transfer to paper towels for another minute and then to cookie racks to cool.   *Yield: 2½ dozen*

JANICE STANGLAND
CEDAR RAPIDS, IOWA

SPECIAL OCCASION CHOCOLATE CHIP COOKIES

The final selection of recipes are for those times when you feel expansive and really want to gild the lily. Many of them are no more difficult to make than any others in this book, but because of their special ingredients, such as imported chocolates or fancy liqueurs, they may tend to be more expensive. Some are the sort that are fun to experiment with when you have some extra time and feel like being creative in the kitchen. They also tend to be extravagant in their supply of calories, with no stinting of chocolate, butter, eggs, and spirits.

Have fun!

CHOCOLATE CHIP MERINGUES

With crisp outsides and delicious, chewy insides, these bars are well worth the calories! To maintain crispness, be sure to store airtight, particularly in humid weather, to maintain crispness.

2 cups flour
1 teaspoon baking powder
¼ teaspoon baking soda
1 cup butter
½ cup granulated sugar

1½ cups light brown sugar, firmly packed and divided
2 eggs, separated
1 teaspoon vanilla extract
12 ounces (2 cups) semisweet chocolate chips
½ cup grated coconut (optional)

Sift together flour, baking powder, and baking soda; set aside.

Cream butter, granulated sugar, and ½ cup brown sugar. Beat in egg yolks. Gradually add dry ingredients, mixing well. Stir in vanilla.

Spread dough onto 9 x 15-inch baking sheet. Sprinkle with chocolate chips and press them into dough.

Beat egg whites until stiff. Gradually add remaining brown sugar, continuing to beat until well mixed. Spread meringue over cookie dough. Sprinkle with coconut.

Bake at 350°F. for 25 minutes. Cut into squares when cool. *Yield: 12 large or 24 small bars*

ANN MARIE McCRYSTAL
VERO BEACH, FLORIDA

BROWNIE CHIP MERINGUES

Chewy chocolate and nuts enveloped in an airy meringue for a festive treat.

15 ounces (2½ cups) semisweet chocolate chips,
   divided
4 egg whites
⅛ teaspoon salt

1 teaspoon vanilla extract
1 teaspoon cider vinegar
1 cup sugar
1 cup chopped walnuts or pecans

Carefully melt 2 cups of the chocolate chips and set aside to cool.

Beat egg whites with salt, vanilla, and vinegar until the mixture stands in soft peaks. Gradually add sugar, beating until stiff peaks form.

Fold in melted chocolate, the remaining chocolate chips, and nuts.

Drop by tablespoons onto greased baking sheets. Bake at 350°F. for about 10 minutes. Do not overbake. Store in airtight cookie tins. *Yield: 6 dozen*

MARGARET A. LANE
VERSAILLES, KENTUCKY

OLD VIENNA CHIP COOKIES

Poppy seeds, cinnamon, apple, walnuts, currants, and chocolate—all chosen to conjure memories of favorite Viennese pastries.

1¼ cups flour
½ teaspoon baking soda
¼ teaspoon salt
½ cup butter
1 cup sugar
1 egg
½ teaspoon cinnamon

½ teaspoon grated lemon zest
2 tablespoons poppy seeds
¼ cup unpeeled, grated, tart apple
9 ounces (1½ cups) semisweet chocolate chips
¼ cup chopped walnuts
¼ cup currants

Sift flour, baking soda, and salt, and set aside. Cream butter. Gradually add sugar, and beat until creamy. Beat in egg, cinnamon, lemon zest, poppy seeds, and apple. Stir in sifted ingredients and mix well. Gently stir in chocolate chips, nuts, and currants.

Drop batter by teaspoonfuls onto greased baking sheets, placing cookies well apart. Bake at 375°F. for about 10 minutes.   *Yield: 3 dozen*

ROXANNE E. CHAN
ALBANY, CALIFORNIA

APPLE-KISSED CHOCOLATE CHIP COOKIES

For special occasions, try dipping cool cookies first into melted semisweet chocolate, then into a mixture of crushed apple-cinnamon chips and ground nuts.

2 cups flour
1 teaspoon baking soda
1 teaspoon salt
½ cup quick-cooking rolled oats
½ teaspoon cinnamon
¼ cup minced dried apples
½ cup butter
½ cup shortening

¾ cup granulated sugar
¾ cup brown sugar, firmly packed
1 egg
1 egg yolk
½ teaspoon vanilla extract
1½ tablespoons apple brandy
1 cup coarsely chopped nuts
6 ounces (1 cup) semisweet chocolate chips

Sift together flour, baking soda, and salt. Add oats, cinnamon, and dried apples, and mix thoroughly. Set aside.

Cream together well the butter, shortening, and sugars. Add egg, egg yolk, vanilla, and apple brandy, and beat until well blended. Add sifted ingredients, and mix well. Stir in nuts and chocolate chips until well distributed.

Drop dough by large tablespoonfuls onto greased baking sheets, placing cookies about 3 inches apart. To give cookies a more uniform appearance, flatten them slightly with the bottom of a glass dipped in sugar. Bake at 350°F. for 9 to 12 minutes, using the longer baking time for a crisper cookie. Cool on pans for 2 or 3 minutes before removing to racks. *Yield: about 3 dozen*

CHERRY C. QUEEN
SAN ANTONIO, TEXAS

DERBY CHIP DELIGHTS

From Kentucky Derby country comes this bourbon-flavored cookie, rich in brown sugar, chocolate, and nuts. For a somewhat heartier cookie, add ¼ cup whole wheat flour, an additional ¼ cup all-purpose flour, and 2 more tablespoons bourbon.

2¼ cups flour, unsifted
1 teaspoon baking soda
½ teaspoon salt
1 cup margarine, softened
¾ cup granulated sugar

¾ cup brown sugar, firmly packed
5 tablespoons bourbon
2 eggs
1½ cups milk chocolate chips
1½ cups walnuts, chopped

Sift together the flour, baking soda, and salt; set aside.

Cream margarine with the sugars. Beat in bourbon and eggs. Stir in sifted ingredients. Gently stir in chocolate chips and walnuts.

Drop by teaspoonfuls onto lightly greased baking sheets. Bake at 350°F. for 10 minutes, or until cookie is light brown. Remove from pans while still warm.   *Yield: about 6 dozen*

LEAH HUFF
LOUISVILLE, KENTUCKY

CLIPPER CHOCOLATE CHIPPER

This is an adaptation of a cookie served on a Caribbean Island cruise ship. Serve warm from the oven to bring out the hazelnut and coffee flavors of the Frangelico and Tia Maria liqueurs.

1 cup granulated sugar
1 cup brown sugar
2 cups butter
1½ tablespoons baking soda
¼ cup Frangelico liqueur
¼ cup Tia Maria liqueur

1 tablespoon salt
3 eggs
6 cups pastry flour
24 ounces (4 cups) semisweet chocolate chips
¼ cup pecans, chopped
¼ cup walnuts, chopped

Cream together the sugars, butter, baking soda, liqueurs, and salt until light and creamy. Add eggs, beating after each addition until well blended.

Stir in flour, chocolate chips, and nuts, and mix until well blended.

Drop by tablespoons onto greased baking sheets. Flatten slightly with moistened fingers or back of spoon. Bake at 350°F. for 8 to 10 minutes, or until golden brown.   *Yield: 4 dozen*

LELIA N. HILLGER
ST. LOUIS, MISSOURI

CREAMY DELIGHTFUL CHIP

Irish Mist and chocolate—the two smooth tastes are elegantly complementary. And for the ultimate antedote to a cold, damp winter's day, serve a batch of these fresh from the oven with a pot of tea enhanced by a splash of Irish Mist.

2½ cups flour
1 teaspoon baking soda
½ teaspoon salt
1 cup margarine, softened
¼ cup granulated sugar
1 cup brown sugar, firmly packed

1 egg, beaten
1 8-ounce package cream cheese, softened
12 ounces (2 cups) semisweet chocolate chips, divided
¼ cup Irish Mist
1 cup pecans, chopped

Sift together flour, baking soda, and salt, and set aside.

Cream margarine and sugars together well. Add egg and mix well. Add sifted ingredients to margarine mixture.

In a glass bowl in the microwave or in a small pan on the stove heat cream cheese and ⅓ of the chocolate chips until soft. Add Irish Mist to chocolate and cheese mixture. Add all of this to the first mixture. Gently stir in the rest of the chocolate chips and the nuts.

Drop by teaspoonfuls onto lightly greased cookie sheet. Bake at 375°F. for 8 to 10 minutes. *Yield: 8 dozen*

KATHY YORK
LOUISVILLE, KENTUCKY

CABLE CAR CHOCOLATE WHEELS

*Serve as a special dessert topped with chocolate ice cream, hot fudge sauce,
whipped cream, and chocolate sprinkles.*

3 cups flour
2 teaspoons baking soda
1½ teaspoons salt
½ cup graham cracker crumbs (about 3½ whole
   crackers)
1 cup margarine
½ cup unsalted (sweet) butter

1½ cups granulated sugar
1 cup light brown sugar, firmly packed
4 eggs
2 tablespoons Grand Marnier or amaretto liqueur
12 ounces (2 cups) semisweet chocolate chips
2 cups chopped mixed nuts

Combine flour, baking soda, salt, and graham cracker crumbs, and set aside.

In a large bowl, combine margarine, butter, and sugars, and beat with an electric mixer at high speed until light and fluffy (about 5 minutes). Add eggs, one at a time, beating well after each addition. Add liqueur. Mix dry ingredients into creamed mixture until well blended. Stir in chocolate chips and nuts by hand.

Drop by scant ¼ cupfuls onto lightly greased baking sheets, placing cookies about 3 inches apart. Bake at 350°F. for 16 to 18 minutes, or until golden brown. Watch carefully; cookies brown very quickly. Transfer to racks to cool.
Yield: about 3½ dozen

IRENE E. SOUZA
SUNNYVALE, CALIFORNIA

TASTE-OF-SUMMER CHOCOLATE CHIP COOKIES

*Peach schnapps, a hint of almond, the nutlike wholesomeness of rolled oats—
and chocolate, of course.*

2½ cups flour
1 teaspoon baking soda
1 teaspoon salt
1 cup butter or margarine, softened
¾ cup granulated sugar
¾ cup plus 2 tablespoons light brown sugar, firmly
  packed

2 eggs
1½ teaspoons vanilla extract
½ teaspoon almond extract
⅓ cup peach schnapps
12 ounces (2 cups) semisweet chocolate chips
1 cup quick-cooking rolled oats

Combine flour, baking soda, and salt, and set aside.

Cream butter and sugars. Add eggs, vanilla and almond extracts, and schnapps, and beat well. Gradually add dry ingredients, blending well. Stir in chocolate chips and oats.

Drop by rounded teaspoonfuls onto lightly greased baking sheets. Bake at 350°F. for about 10 to 12 minutes, or until very lightly browned. Remove from baking sheets to cool.   *Yield: about 2½ dozen*

LINDA J. KICK
CAMILLUS, NEW YORK

CRÈME DE CHIP COOKIES

English walnuts may be used in place of black walnuts, of course, but if you are lucky enough to live where black walnut trees are abundant, you will enjoy their distinctive flavor, here further enhanced by chocolate and crème de cacao.

12 ounces (2 cups) semisweet chocolate chips
½ cup crème de cacao, divided
1¾ cups flour
1½ teaspoons baking powder
¼ teaspoon salt (optional)

1 cup brown sugar, firmly packed
⅓ cup vegetable oil
2 eggs, beaten
1 cup coarsely chopped black walnuts
1 cup confectioners' sugar

Soak chocolate chips in the crème de cacao for about 30 minutes.

While the chips are soaking, sift together flour, baking powder, and salt, and set aside.

Drain crème de cacao from chips and save. Combine 1 cup of the chips, ¼ cup of the crème de cacao, brown sugar, and oil in a deep saucepan. Cook over medium-low heat, stirring constantly until chips are melted. Remove from heat.

Add eggs and beat well. Beat in sifted ingredients until thoroughly mixed. Add nuts and remaining chips and creme de cacao; mix well.

Chill dough for about an hour, or until it can be formed into balls with your hands.

Form teaspoonfuls into small loose balls. Roll balls in confectioners' sugar, and place about 2 inches apart on lightly greased baking sheets. Bake at 350°F. for 10 to 12 minutes. Remove from pans to cool completely. Store airtight.
Yield: 6 to 7 dozen

PATRICIA NEAVES
KANSAS CITY, MISSOURI

KAHLUA COCONUT CHOCOLATE CHIP COOKIES

Kahlua, with its coffee and molasses flavors, and coconut make an interesting complement to chocolate.

2¼ cups flour
1 teaspoon baking soda
⅔ cup butter, softened
¼ cup granulated sugar
¾ cup light brown sugar, firmly packed
⅓ cup Kahlua

1 package (4-serving size) vanilla-flavor instant pudding mix
2 eggs
12 ounces (2 cups) semisweet chocolate chips
1 cup chopped pecans
½ cup flaked coconut

Mix together flour and baking soda, and set aside.

In a large mixing bowl, combine butter, sugars, Kahlua, and pudding mix, and beat until smooth and creamy. Beat in eggs. Gradually blend in dry ingredients, then the chocolate chips, nuts, and coconut. Chill dough for 1 to 2 hours.

Form dough into walnut-sized balls, or drop by rounded teaspoonfuls onto ungreased baking sheets. Bake at 375°F. for about 9 minutes. *Yield: 5 dozen*

KATHLEEN A. ROSEBROUGH
SOUTHFIELD, MICHIGAN

GRAND MARNIER CHOCOLATE CHIP COOKIES

The sophisticated tastes of Grand Marnier, itself orange flavored, and orange peel cut the sugary sweetness of the traditional cookie.

2½ cups flour
2 teaspoons baking powder
¼ teaspoon salt
1 cup margarine
½ cup granulated sugar
¾ cup brown sugar, firmly packed
2 eggs, well-beaten
1½ tablespoons Grand Marnier

1 tablespoon grated orange peel
12 ounces (2 cups) semisweet chocolate chips
1 cup chopped walnuts

Glaze:
6 ounces semisweet baking chocolate
1 tablespoon Grand Marnier
½ cup finely chopped walnuts

Sift flour before measuring, then resift with baking powder and salt; set aside.

Cream margarine and sugars until light and fluffy. Add eggs, and blend well. Add sifted ingredients to creamed mixture together with Grand Marnier and orange peel. Mix thoroughly. Fold in chocolate chips and nuts.

Drop by rounded teaspoonfuls onto ungreased baking sheets. Bake at 325°F. for about 20 minutes. Remove from pans and cool completely.

For glaze, melt chocolate in a double boiler over hot, but not boiling, water. Remove from heat and beat in Grand Marnier. Coat undersides of cool cookies with chocolate glaze, then dip in chopped nuts. Refrigerate a few minutes until firm. Glaze may also be poured in stripes over top of cookies, omitting nuts. *Yield: about 4 dozen*

AINSLIE BRUNEAU
LEE, MASSACHUSETTS

CHOCOLATE CHIP ALMOND COOKIES

This candylike cookie features a sugary, almond coating.

3½ cups flour
1 teaspoon baking soda
1 teaspoon salt
1 teaspoon cream of tartar
1 cup butter, softened
1 cup granulated sugar
1 cup light brown sugar, *not* packed
1 cup vegetable oil
1 egg

1 teaspoon vanilla extract
2 teaspoons amaretto liqueur
1 cup rolled oats
8 ounces milk chocolate, grated
12 ounces (2 cups) semisweet chocolate minichips
3 cups chopped almonds
6 tablespoons confectioners' sugar
2 egg whites, beaten slightly

Combine flour, baking soda, salt, and cream of tartar, and set aside.

In large mixer bowl, cream together butter and sugars. Blend in oil, egg, vanilla, and amaretto. Gradually add dry ingredients, along with rolled oats, until well blended. Gently stir in grated milk chocolate and chocolate chips. Chill until firm.

Mix together chopped almonds and powdered sugar. Form dough into 1-inch balls. Dip balls into beaten egg white, then roll them in almond-sugar mixture. Place on lightly greased baking sheets. Bake at 375°F. for 8 to 10 minutes. Cool slightly before removing to cooling racks. *Yield: 8 to 9 dozen*

BOB AND CARLA WITMER
COLORADO SPRINGS, COLORADO

TOP HAT CHOCOLATE CHIPS

A bar cookie topped with chocolate-flavored cream cheese, nuts, and chocolate chips.

2 cups flour
1 teaspoon baking soda
1⅔ cups sugar, divided
2 eggs
¾ cup water
⅓ cup oil
1 teaspoon vanilla extract

16 ounces cream cheese, softened to room
  temperature
¼ cup unsweetened cocoa
½ teaspoon salt
1 cup chopped nuts
12 ounces (2 cups) semisweet chocolate chips

Mix together flour, baking soda, and 1 cup sugar. Add *1* egg, water, oil, and vanilla, and stir until well blended.

Spread batter on 15 x 10-inch greased baking sheet. Bake at 350° F. for 15 minutes.

While this is baking, combine cream cheese, remaining sugar, cocoa, salt, and the other egg; cream well. At the end of the 15-minute baking period, spread cheese mixture over hot base, and return pan to oven; continue to bake for another 15 minutes. Remove from oven and while still hot, sprinkle nuts and chips over all. Cut into squares.

You may form cookie "sandwiches" by placing squares on top of each other, cheese sides facing, while they are still warm. Cool completely before storing in refrigerator. *Yield: 2 to 3 dozen*

HILDA GAREY
ST. ALBANS, VERMONT

CREAM CHEESE & CHOCOLATE CHIP WHEELS

Inspired by a love for truffles, this is the cookie to bake on a day when you have time on your hands and feel like being creative in the kitchen.

8 ounces cream cheese, very cold and firm, divided
7 tablespoons confectioners' sugar
1½ cups flour
½ teaspoon baking soda
¼ teaspoon salt
½ cup butter, softened to room temperature
½ cup chunky peanut butter, room temperature
¼ cup granulated sugar
½ cup brown sugar, firmly packed
2 jumbo eggs, beaten
1 teaspoon vanilla extract
1 teaspoon rum flavoring
¾ cup black walnuts, finely chopped
12 ounces (2 cups) semisweet chocolate chips, divided
2 tablespoons unsweetened cocoa

Set aside 4 ounces of cream cheese to soften to room temperature.

On an 18-inch strip of waxed paper sprinkle 4 tablespoons of confectioners' sugar down the center in a line about 3 inches wide by 12 inches long. Cut the cold cream cheese into four 1-ounce strips. Place pieces end to end along the line of sugar. Reaching underneath the waxed paper, roll the pieces of cheese over the sugar to coat them completely and form a long roll of sugared cheese. Continue rolling inside the waxed paper until cheese is about ½ to ¾ inch in diameter. Place roll of cheese in refrigerator to keep cold and firm.

Mix together the flour, baking soda, and salt, and set aside.

Combine butter, peanut butter, sugars, and remaining 4 ounces of softened cream cheese, and cream well.

Mix flavorings with beaten eggs, and beat into creamed mixture until well blended. Stir in the dry ingredients. Stir in the nuts and all but ¼ cup of chocolate chips. Refrigerate dough at least 30 minutes.

Mix together the cocoa and the remaining confectioners' sugar. Drop heaping tablespoonfuls of the chilled dough into cocoa mixture, and roll to coat the outside; be careful not to allow the cocoa to become *mixed with* the dough. Place coated cookie balls onto ungreased baking sheet, and flatten to about ½ inch thickness with bottom of a glass.

Slice off ¼-inch thick pieces of chilled cream cheese roll, and press one slice flat into the center of each cookie. Allow cookies to set for about 15 minutes. Next press a chocolate chip, point end down, into each cream cheese center so that flat bottom of chip extends slightly above cheese. (Small pieces of black walnut can be substituted for chocolate chips.)

Bake at 350°F. for 12 minutes. Allow to cool on pans for about 4 minutes before removing to racks to cool thoroughly.   *Yield: 4 dozen*

BETTY JANE ROBINSON
STILLWATER, OKLAHOMA

INDEX

A

Aging of chocolate, 14
Almond extract, 44, 45, 58, 83, 100, 130
Almonds, 22, 53, 83, 134
Amaretto liqueur, 129, 134
American Enterpreneurs Association, 10
Apple(s)
  brandy, 125
  butter, 71
  recipes using, 71, 124, 125
Apricot preserves, 69
Apricots, 56, 69, 107
Artificial chocolate, 15

B

Baking chocolate, 14
  semisweet, 133
  sweet, 80
Baking cookies, 28-29, 31
Baking parchment, 25
Bittersweet chocolate, 15, 120
Bloom, 16
Bourbon, 126
Bran, 90
  flakes, 105
Breakfast cocoa, 14
Burning of cookies, preventing, 29
Butter, choosing type of, 18
Buttermilk, 22, 60
Butterscotch chips, 83

C

Cacao tree, 14
Cashews, 52
Chocolate
  artificial, 15
  baking, 14
  bittersweet, 15, 120
  conching, 14
  dark, 15
  drink, 7
  flavored, 15
  freezing of, 16
  history of, 7-10, 14
  how to choose, 17
  how to make, 14
  how to substitute cocoa for, 15
  ice cream, 118
  liquor, 14
  melting of, 16-17
  milk, 8, 15, 17, 46, 47, 49, 51, 52, 58, 74, 81, 82, 83, 98, 101, 105, 126, 134
  mixing, 27
  process for making bars of, 8
  refining, 14
  semisweet baking, 133
  sizes to use, 17
  storing, 15-16
  sweet baking, 80
  sweet dark, 15
  syrups, 15
  unsweetened, 120

Chocolate (continued)
  white, 15, 17, 46, 48, 51, 117
Cider vinegar, 123
Cinnamon, 7, 64, 65, 66, 108, 124, 125
Cloves, 64, 103, 108
Cocoa
  breakfast, 14
  butter/fat, 14, 16
  Dutch-processed, 14
  how to substitute, for chocolate, 15
  instant, 15
  powder, 14
  recipes using, 6, 74, 107, 110, 111-114, 116-119, 135, 136
  storing, 16
Coconut
  cream, 75
  flaked, 45, 47, 48, 74, 75, 91, 96, 105, 106, 132
  flavoring, 83
  grated, 122
  shredded, 95, 104
Coffee granules, 79, 107
Conching, 14
Confectioners' chocolate, 15
Confectioners' sugar, 66, 131, 134, 136
Corn flakes, 104, 105
Corn oil, 43, 93
Cornstarch, 21
Corn syrup, 19, 31, 46, 58, 59, 112
Cream cheese, 119, 128, 135, 136
Creaming butter/margarine, 27

Cream of tartar, 21-22, 120, 134
Crème de cacao, 131
Crème de menthe candy, 53
Currants, 124

D
Dark chocolate, 15
David's Cookie Kitchens, 10
Dough
   chilling, 27-28
   forming, 28
   freezing, 28
   ingredients for, 18-19
   mixing, 26-27
Drop cookies, 28
Dry ingredients, mixing, 26, 27
Dutch-processed cocoa, 14

E
Eggs
   adding, 19, 27
   adding yolk, 31

F
Famous Amos, 10
Filberts. *See* Hazelnuts
Flour
   choosing type of, 20-21
   sifting of, 20, 26
Forming cookies, 28
Frangelico liqueur, 127
Freezing
   chocolate, 16
   cookies, 30
   dough, 28
Fructose, 74

G
Ginger, 64, 65, 66, 103, 108
Graham cracker crumbs, 129

Grand Marnier, 129, 133

H
Hazelnut butter, 85
Hazelnuts, 22, 105
Hershey's Kisses, 17
Honey, 19, 31, 64, 68, 72, 88, 107
Hot peppers, 7

I
Ingredients, mixing of, 26-27
Irish Mist, 128

K
Kahlua, 132

L
Leavening, 21-22
Lemon zest, 124

M
Macadamias, 10, 47, 48, 52
M&Ms, 17
Maple syrup, 73
Margarine
   substituting for butter, 18
   whipped, 18
Melting chocolate, 16-17
Milk
   condensed, 8
   dry, 106
   powdered, 88
   recipes using, 15, 50, 59, 70, 110
Milk chocolate, 8, 15, 17
   recipes using, 46, 47, 49, 51, 52, 58, 74, 81-83, 98, 101, 105, 125, 134
Mint-chocolate morsels, 55
Molasses, 19, 22, 70, 78, 103
Mrs. Field's, 10

N
Nestlé Company, 8-9
Nutmeg, 65, 108

O
Oats, rolled, 21
   recipes using, 64, 91-107, 120, 125, 130, 134
Oil, 135
Orange
   extract, 108
   juice, 67
   peel, 68, 133
   zest, 67
Oven, preheating of, 26

P
Pans, choosing, 25
Peach schnapps, 130
Peanut butter, 6
   recipes using, 82, 84, 85, 96, 102, 106, 136
Peanut butter chips, 54, 84
Peanuts, salted, 104
Pecans, 44, 45, 49, 51, 52, 55, 59, 66, 75, 78, 79, 83, 84, 90, 101, 110, 111, 115, 116, 119, 123, 127, 128, 132
Pinto beans, 107
Poppy seeds, 124
Potato chips, 63
Pumpkin purée, 65

R
Raisins, 55, 57, 96, 101, 103
Rice cereal, 62
Rolled oats. *See* Oats, rolled
Rum flavoring, 136